MARY EMMERLING'S

AMERICAN
COUNTRY COOKING

MARY EMMERLING'S
AMERICAN COUNTRY COOKING

RECIPES AND MENUS FROM
FAMILY AND FRIENDS ACROSS AMERICA

Photographs by Michael Skott
Design by Drenttel Doyle Partners

CLARKSON N. POTTER, INC. / PUBLISHERS
DISTRIBUTED BY CROWN PUBLISHERS, INC. NEW YORK

The photographs that appear on pages i, vii, 66, 67 (above), and 68 are reprinted by permission from HOUSE BEAUTIFUL, copyright © November 1984. The Hearst Corporation. All Rights Reserved. Michael Skott, photographer.

Grateful acknowledgment is given for the five recipes appearing on pages 76 and 77, from *The Loaves and Fishes Cookbook*. Copyright © 1985 by Anna Pump and Gen Le Roy. Reprinted by permission of Macmillan Publishing Company.

Published by Clarkson N. Potter, Inc., 225 Park Avenue South, New York, New York 10003, and represented in Canada by the Canadian MANDA Group

CLARKSON N. POTTER, POTTER, and colophon are trademarks of Clarkson N. Potter, Inc.

Manufactured in Japan

Library of Congress Cataloging-in-Publication Data

Emmerling, Mary Ellisor.
Mary Emmerling's American country cooking.

Includes index.
1. Cookery, American.   2. Menus.   I. Title.
II. Title: American country cooking.
TX715.E534   1987   641.5973   86-22522
ISBN 0-517-56020-8

10 9 8 7 6 5 4 3 2 1
First Edition

To *my mother,
Marthena Ellisor, and her favorite
recipes, which are now mine,
Samantha's, and Jonathan's.*

▲ ▲ ▲ ▲ ▲

*To my brother, Terry Ellisor, for his
terrific Margaritas, Champagne and
caviar, and tunafish sandwiches.*

❧

*And, always, to Chris Mead,
for all the great entertaining we
have done together.*

♥

ACKNOWLEDGMENTS

Since I travel so much of the year, the nicest invitation I can receive is for a home-cooked meal. During all my traveling days as an editor at *Mademoiselle* and *House Beautiful* and while working on *American Country, Collecting American Country,* and *American Country West,* the best food and times have been at home with friends.

Whether the meal was casual or formal, what impressed me the most was that there was always something special prepared. There never seemed to be any trouble getting the food ready and on the table, and sometimes everyone just pitched in, setting the table, opening the wine. It was like part of the conversation, effortless and fun!

My friends make it all look easy, natural, and pretty. They don't wait for a special occasion to use their good china and silver. Any time you come to their homes, you're the special occasion!

There's something comforting, inspired, and wonderful about the way my friends open their houses and their arms to guests, the way they set their tables and serve up delicious food. This book presents their regional and family recipes, as well as their own personal favorites. It welcomes you to their homes and gardens, and shows you how they live and entertain.

American Country Cooking is my way of thanking my friends by telling them they're so special I want to share them with you.

I am also grateful to the friends who helped put this book together: Susan and Clint Rodenberg; Baby Jo and Okaree Willingham; Horst K. Klein, Design Cuisine, of Fairfax, Virginia; Mel Fillini; and Bob Thixton.

And, always, my good friends in New York City who support me: Jody Greif, who has been so helpful with the whole book, especially with my traveling and the directory; Mardee Regan, a lover of good food who has tested every recipe; Carol Sama Sheehan, whose wonderful writing puts my words and stories into order; Stephen Doyle and Rosemarie Sohmer, whose details and design brought the book together; to Pam Reycraft for all her assistance; and, finally, to my photographer, Michael Skott, for his beautiful pictures and for traveling America with me.

Special thanks also to some friends along the way who taught me a lot about entertaining: Mary Cantwell, whose "Eat" column at *Mademoiselle* was my favorite, and Dona Guimaraes, whose entertaining style is so special.

And to my kids, Jonathan and Samantha, who can always be found in the

kitchen baking chocolate chip cookies or popovers or mixing a great vinaigrette. It is never too early to start! My favorite is breakfast in bed for Mother's Day, which has become a family tradition.

And, always, to Juanita Jones for *all* she does for me and my children.

W*ith very special thanks to:*

Cheri and Bobby Carter, and all the guests at the Potluck Dinner; Beverly and David Cummings; Dick Duane; Ken Dudwick, Paul Drymalski, and Libby Dollahon; Nora Jane and Tammy Etheridge; Priscilla Hoback and Peter Gould; Marilyn and John Hannigan; Mary and Ed Higgins; Elaine and Arnie Horwitch; Lyn Hutchings; Beverly and Tommy Jacomini; Sue Ellen and Steve Johnson; Audrey and Doug Julian; Barbara and Norman Kaufman; Don Kelly and Warren Fitzsimmons; Kathy and John Killip; Bobbie and Dub King; Gaye Kleweno; Libby and Dick Kramer; Charleen Kress; Senator Paul Laxalt and his wife, Carol; Carol Leverett; Loaves & Fishes; Rosalea Murphy; Cynthia Pedregon, Ottis and Sally Layne, Juli Dodds, Carol Bade, and Joan Harris; Nancy and Derek Power; Tom Reeves; Nancy Reynolds; Jackie and Bob Rose; Marsha Sands of the Cameleon's Restaurant; Vicky, Pat, and George Van Harlingen; Evangeline Washington; Lynn and Don Watt; Corrie and Bill Wickens; Sudie Woodson.

I will always be grateful to Gayle Benderoff and Deborah Geltman, my wonderful agents, and to all my friends and supporters at Clarkson N. Potter and Crown Publishers. First, to Nancy Novogrod, who is still the best editor—forever! To Carol Southern, Editorial Director of Potter, a great supporter of Country; Nat Wartels, Chairman of Crown Publishers, Alan Mirken, President, and Bruce Harris, Vice-President and Director of Publishing; Gael Towey, for her great art direction, and Jonathan Fox for helping Nancy and me; Laurie Stark, Ann S. Cahn, and Joan Denman; Michelle Sidrane, Phyllis Fleiss, and Jo Fagan, in Subrights; Nancy Kahan, Barbara Marks, and Susan Butler in Publicity, who keep me on the road—all the time; Gail Shanks and everyone else on the Crown Publishers sales force who make all my books big sellers.

So invite some people over, have a good time, and always take pleasure in entertaining your family and friends.

Mary Emmerling
January 1987

CONTENTS

Crisscrossing the United States as often as I do, compiling material for my books, I have discovered that the warmth of Country style goes far beyond baskets hanging from the rafters, layers of quilts and Indian blankets on handcrafted beds, or Country cupboards brimming with family treasures. Country style really has more to do with the feeling of home than the objects that are in it. Nowhere is this attitude better expressed than at the family table, in the simplicity and flavor of American cooking as varied as a lobster boil in Maine, a German-style pork roast dinner in Pennsylvania, or a light pasta supper dressed with a simple sauce of ripe tomatoes in California's fertile Napa Valley.

I know from experience the comfort of the kitchen. In every house I've lived in, I've never been able to keep guests out of this room. The first thing I did when I moved to New York was put a big Country table smack in the middle of my East Side kitchen, not exactly in line with the chrome and glass look that was then popular. But a funny thing happened when friends came over for dinner: They never wanted to leave this table, even after sitting for hours in rustic ladderback chairs. Everyone felt at home there.

Back then, my cooking repertoire was slender, but I always made a fuss over the table and grew pots of herbs to add a touch of freshness to carry-out entrées that came to the rescue of this young, working mother. Home became the gathering place for friends when my children, Samantha and Jonathan, were toddlers. My Country-in-the-City style helped me create a comfortable setting for the informal Emmerling dinners that were regular Saturday night events.

At this time, my interest in collecting Americana was growing rapidly. A trip to a local flea market would often produce the inspiration for an evening's meal, like finding a great old wooden bowl or Shaker basket and then coming home and making something special to put in it. Then, as my collecting became a career, and my travels stretched across the United States, I began to meet people, like myself, who connected with "Country" in a special way that was reflected not only in the things they collected but in the way they lived, and perhaps more important, in how they welcomed guests into their homes.

Although these friends were busy people with schedules that read like complicated timetables, they found time at the end of a day to make a new

visitor feel like family. I'll never forget the hospitality of Beverly Jacomini, who extended to me the use of her beautiful farmhouse *even* before we had ever met. She drove an hour and a half from Houston and an hour and a half back in order to take me to dinner at her husband's Texas roadside café The Hofbrau, when, after asking me what I'd like to have for dinner, I responded, "A big Texas steak."

All my friends in this Country network exude the same enthusiasm for meeting people and exchanging information about what they love most—American Country. Whether a wonderful resource for locally made rustic furniture or a family's treasured recipe for old-fashioned meat loaf, the sharing of Country secrets is our bond.

Family traditions and regional tastes merge in the area of the American Country cooking that this book celebrates. Just as the homes of my friends reflect a country simplicity, so does the food they cook. It is tied to the apron strings of treasured family recipes, handed down like heirlooms, and to the availability of garden-fresh fruits and vegetables like those first cultivated by America's early settlers.

By "cuisine," I don't mean fancy. Many of these cooks are classically trained—graduates of such legendary cooking schools as the Cordon Bleu and La Varenne. They bring the taste and flair of experienced cooks to preparing their favorite simple Country recipes.

Throughout the book, menus reflect

the abundance of the American marketplace from the fashionable king salmon of the Pacific Northwest to rosy red tomatoes and the universal string bean. Homely it may be but, with garnishes such as the chanterelle mushrooms one California cook uses, or pimientos another friend likes to carve

into heart shapes, the common green bean receives an uncommon treatment in the Country kitchen. It is no secret that I can't resist anything heart-shaped, and I was especially pleased to find heart-shaped muffins, cakes, even a casserole topped with a paprika heart, welcoming me. This symbol seemed as emblematic to Country tables as the baskets, blue and white tableware, and homespun linens that decorate them.

Country tables are casual, yet elegant, and American Country Cooking rejoices in the special settings in which we serve our recipes. A fish supper in Ohio is enjoyed on the banks of a rural pond on new pewter plates laid out on a table decorated with wild flower bouquets. An early summer luncheon is served on a back porch in the Blue Ridge Mountains with white wicker furniture and antique table linens. An intimate dinner in a California courtyard transports guests to faraway Tuscany, Italy, where the hostess perfected her cooking techniques.

Visiting the friends I have made and experiencing their enthusiasm for entertaining has been my pleasure. I hope the Country secrets they have so generously shared with me will bring the spirit and goodness of *American Country Cooking* into your home.

MARY EMMERLING'S

AMERICAN
COUNTRY COOKING

EARLY SPRING IN MISSISSIPPI

Rockport, Mississippi

*Nora Jane cuts fresh flowers for
the table from her country garden
(above). The house with its
welcoming porch (left) evolved
from a pair of log cabins built in
the 1800s.*

For me, the year begins in the spring, when the country comes alive again with flowers and I think of the fun of being outdoors with friends in good weather and the luscious fresh fruits and vegetables that the earth's goodness will soon provide. Spring appears early in Mississippi, so that on my March visit with good friends Nora Jane and Tammy Etheridge, I was able to partake of many of these pleasures.

Some fifty miles south of Jackson (the state capital, where the family maintains its principal residence) in a simple cabin free of telephones and television, the Etheridges treat their friends to the uncomplicated and informal entertaining style that Nora Jane, a lifelong southerner, likes best. Curtainless windows usher in the breeze, fireplaces warm the bedrooms, and roomy rocking chairs on the front porch await the arrival of guests. "There's not a lot to fuss with in this kind of house," says Nora Jane, who gathers her own bouquets from flowers in her cutting garden and wild flowers in nearby fields.

Here in the country, guests feel right

Whether dressed in a flaky pastry crust or in symbolic form as table decorations (above), chicken appears regularly on the table at the Etheridges', whose family business is raising poultry. By the front door, a plaque (right) attests to the landmark status of the house.

ALFORD-LITTLE HOUSE
PLACED ON THE

**NATIONAL REGISTER
OF HISTORIC PLACES**

BY THE UNITED STATES
DEPARTMENT OF THE INTERIOR

M E N U

LUNCH

Mississippi Pimm's Cup

Chicken Pie

Marinated Tomatoes

Asparagus Vinaigrette

Strawberry Ice Cream

*Iced Tea with Lemon
Wedges and Fresh Mint*

3

at home, pitching in to make the salad or wash the dishes. "It's just that kind of a setting," Nora Jane observes. "This house is exactly the way it's always been and that's its charm."

Rockport itself is a relatively small town, located on the Pearl River in an area where poultry, hogs, cotton, and sweet potatoes are important cash crops. There's plenty of game in the surrounding woodlands and no shortage of catfish in the lakes, ponds, and streams. Buttermilk biscuits, chicken pot pie, country ham from peanut-fed hogs, and pecan pie are among the region's culinary traditions.

Nora Jane and Tammy's country cabin is no grand antebellum house of columns and brick. But a stopover at the Etheridges' offers the warmth and comfort of any Tara, and soul-satisfying food to go with it.

A favorite of England's sporting crowd, the citrus-and-herb spirit of Pimm's Cup is here adapted to southern tastes with the addition of soda and fresh-from-the-orchard cherries.

MISSISSIPPI PIMM'S CUP

1 to 2 parts Pimm's Cup
  Whole strawberries, raspberries,
    cherries, sliced peaches, or sliced
    apples
2 to 3 parts 7-Up or club soda

Mix the Pimm's Cup and fruit in a pitcher and let stand for 30 minutes to 1 hour to allow the flavors to develop. Add soda and pour into glasses filled with ice.

━━━━━ ∞∞∞∞∞ ━━━━━

CHICKEN PIE

Nora Jane's chicken pie is made the old family way. She doesn't "doctor it up"; she just relies on the rich chicken flavor. She cautions everyone not to use boneless chicken breasts; they toughen when simmered.

PASTRY

    3 cups all-purpose flour
    2 teaspoons salt
    1 cup shortening, chilled
    4 to 5 tablespoons ice water

CHICKEN FILLING

    4 whole chicken breasts with skin
        attached, split
    2 garlic cloves, halved
    5 celery stalks with leaves, quartered
    2 carrots, cut into chunks
    1 medium onion, coarsely chopped
      Salt and freshly ground black pepper
    8 tablespoons (1 stick) unsalted butter
    ¼ cup plus 2 tablespoons all-purpose
      flour

Make the pastry: In a large bowl, combine the flour and salt. Using a pastry blender or two knives, cut in the shortening until the mixture resembles coarse meal. One tablespoon at a time, add the ice water, mixing until the pastry forms a ball. Wrap in plastic wrap and refrigerate for at least 30 minutes.

Make the chicken filling: Put the chicken breasts in a large pot along with the garlic, celery, carrots, onion, and salt and pepper to taste. Add enough water to cover. Bring the water to a simmer over high heat. Turn the heat to moderately low and simmer until the chicken is just tender, 25 to 30 minutes.

Using tongs, remove the chicken from the stock and allow it to cool. Raise the heat under the chicken stock and bring it to a boil. Let the stock boil to concentrate the flavors until needed.

Remove and discard the chicken skin and bones and shred the chicken meat or cut it into bite-size pieces. Cover to prevent drying out. Strain the chicken stock and discard the solids. Reserve 4 cups of stock; save the remainder for another use.

In a large saucepan, melt the butter over moderate heat. Add the flour and stir to blend completely. Cook the roux, stirring constantly, over moderate heat for 3 minutes without letting it color. Add the hot chicken stock and stir until the sauce is well combined. Simmer until slightly thickened, about 5 minutes, and set aside.

Preheat the oven to 400°F.

Roll out the pastry and trim it to fit into a shallow 3-quart oval or oblong

casserole dish; reserve the pastry scraps.

Combine the sauce with the shredded chicken and season with salt and pepper to taste. Pour the mixture into the pastry-lined dish.

Roll out the remaining pastry and cut it into ½-inch-wide strips. Cover the pie with the pastry strips, weaving them in a lattice fashion. Trim and crimp the edges.

Place the pie on a baking sheet and bake in the center of the oven for 45 to 55 minutes, or until the pastry is golden brown. Let the pie stand for about 10 minutes before serving.

Serves 12

━━━━━ ∞∞∞∞∞ ━━━━━

MARINATED TOMATOES

Make sure that you use good ripe tomatoes, not those pale orange, flavorless ones. Most farmers' markets, like the one near Nora Jane, carry them flown in from Florida or Mexico almost year-round.

   6 **large ripe tomatoes, peeled**
   ¼ **cup thinly sliced scallions (including**
      some of the green parts)
   ¼ **cup minced fresh parsley**
   1 **garlic clove, minced**
   2 **tablespoons fresh thyme leaves, or ½**
      teaspoon dried thyme
   1 **teaspoon salt**
   ¼ **teaspoon freshly ground black pepper**
   ⅔ **cup vegetable oil**
   ¼ **cup red or white wine vinegar**

Cut the tomatoes into thick slices and put them on a shallow plate.

In a small bowl, combine the scallions, parsley, garlic, thyme, salt, and pepper. Sprinkle the mixture over the tomatoes.

In a jar, mix together the oil and vinegar and pour over the tomatoes. Cover and refrigerate for several hours or overnight, spooning the dressing over the tomatoes from time to time.

Drain off the dressing just before serving.

Serves 6

ASPARAGUS VINAIGRETTE

   1 **pound fresh asparagus spears, steamed**
      and cooled
   Vinaigrette (see page 24)

Arrange the asparagus spears in a shallow bowl.

In a jar, combine the vinaigrette ingredients and shake well. Pour the vinaigrette over the asparagus spears and chill or serve at room temperature.

Serves 4

STRAWBERRY ICE CREAM

Made without the addition of egg yolks and without a cooked custard base, this ice cream is extremely rich and good. If you like, you can use 1 cup heavy cream and ½ cup milk rather than all heavy cream.

   1½ **cups heavy cream**
   ½ **cup crushed strawberries**
   ½ **cup sugar**
   ½ **teaspoon vanilla extract**

In a bowl, combine the cream, strawberries, sugar, and vanilla and stir until the sugar has dissolved.

Pour the mixture into an ice-cream machine and freeze according to the manufacturer's directions.

Makes 1 pint

No fancy presentation is required for homemade strawberry ice cream: a simple glass tumbler and heart-shaped spoon will do (left). Nora Jane would never set a table without first gathering flowers from her gardens and fields for a colorful centerpiece (right).

MENU

DINNER

Southern Fried Chicken

Okra Creole

Fresh Corn Pudding

Buttermilk Biscuits

Sweet Potato Pie

Chilled White Wine

COUNTRY WEEKEND COOKING

Built in the mid-1800s, Nora Jane and Tammy Etheridges' getaway house consists of two identical cabins connected by a breezeway down the middle. "It's called 'dogtrot' style, because a dog can run from the front door to the back door without breaking stride or turning a corner," Nora Jane explains with a laugh. She has left the wood floors bare and limited furnishings to Country chairs and rockers and a few favorite antiques "to keep things relaxed."

The regional favorite of southern fried chicken is served in Sunday best, with fine china and crystal, starched napkins, and family silver, on a 1732 tilt-top table from New England (left). The arched doorway (below) dates from the original house.

Whether for luncheons on the porch or dinners in the dining room, menus rely on fresh foods and include such family favorites as catfish gumbo, sweet potato pie, and, of course, southern fried chicken. "Both my father and husband are major chicken growers, so we serve lots of chicken."

SOUTHERN FRIED CHICKEN

Nora Jane has a way with fried chicken that produces moist, tender pieces that are crispy brown outside. If you're using dark meat, remember that it requires more cooking time.

  Corn oil
1 cup all-purpose flour
  Salt
  Freshly ground black pepper
2 large whole chicken breasts, split

In a large skillet, preferably cast iron, heat 1 to 1½ inches of oil over high heat until it registers 375°F. on a deep-frying thermometer.

Meanwhile, place flour on a shallow plate and season it with salt and pepper. When the oil is hot, dredge the chicken until well coated on all sides. Do not flour the chicken ahead of time.

Place the chicken in the hot oil and cover tightly. Cook for 10 minutes. Uncover and turn the chicken to the other side. Cook, uncovered, until done, about 15 minutes. Do not turn the chicken again and do not overcook it, or the white meat will toughen.

Drain the chicken briefly on paper towels and serve.

Serves 4

OKRA CREOLE

Nora Jane sometimes likes to add some shrimp or chicken to this classic Creole dish and serve it over rice for Sunday night supper.

- 1 pound fresh or thawed frozen okra (If using frozen, buy it cut up.)
- 2 tablespoons safflower oil
- 2 celery stalks, finely chopped
- 1 small onion, chopped
- 2 medium tomatoes, peeled, seeded, and coarsely chopped
- ½ green bell pepper, finely diced
- 1 teaspoon sugar
- ½ teaspoon salt
- Freshly ground black pepper to taste

If using fresh okra, wash and trim the okra and slice it into medium-thin rounds.

In a large skillet, heat the oil over moderately high heat. Add the okra and cook until it is slightly softened. Add the remaining ingredients and cook, stirring, for 5 minutes. If the vegetables seem too dry, add about ⅓ cup water.

Turn the heat to very low and simmer for about 1 hour, or until all of the liquid has been absorbed. Serve hot.

Serves 6 to 8

FRESH CORN PUDDING

When fresh sweet corn is in season, Nora Jane's family and friends adore this simple and tasty way of making corn pudding.

6 ears fresh sweet corn, shucked, or 3
     cups frozen corn kernels, thawed
½ cup heavy cream
½ cup milk
1 tablespoon sugar
½ teaspoon salt
⅛ teaspoon freshly ground white pepper
4 tablespoons (½ stick) unsalted butter,
     melted
3 large eggs

Preheat the oven to 350°F. Butter a 1½-quart casserole.

If using fresh corn, grate the corn into a bowl, catching all of the kernels and liquid. With a teaspoon, scrape the cobs to remove all of the pulp and liquid. If using frozen corn, put it in a bowl.

Add the cream, milk, sugar, salt, and pepper. Stir in the butter. Beat the eggs together until light and lemon-colored and add them to the corn mixture. Stir to combine thoroughly.

Pour the pudding into the prepared casserole and set the casserole in a baking pan. Add hot water to reach halfway up the side of the casserole and bake for 1 hour, or until set and firm. Serve hot or warm.

Serves 6

BUTTERMILK BISCUITS

3 cups cake flour
1 teaspoon salt
1 tablespoon baking powder
½ teaspoon baking soda
6 tablespoons cold shortening
1 cup buttermilk

Preheat the oven to 450°F.

In a bowl, sift together the flour, salt, baking powder, and baking soda. Using a pastry blender or two knives, cut in the shortening until the mixture resembles coarse meal.

Add the buttermilk all at once and mix it in with a fork, working lightly and quickly for no more than 30 seconds. Knead lightly for 30 seconds.

Pat out the dough to a ¼-inch thickness. Cut into rounds with a 2- to 2½-inch cutter and place the biscuits on an ungreased baking sheet. Bake for 12 to 15 minutes, or until golden brown on top.

Makes about 2 dozen

Along the rural byways of the South (below), a sophisticated cuisine has evolved, as in such classic dishes as Okra Creole (left) served in a yellowware bowl.

SWEET POTATO PIE

Though many sweet potato pies are spiced and sweetened, this one is not. Nora Jane will tell you that "if you add anything extra, you'll destroy that sweet potato taste that's so good and so rich." The filling for this pie can be served as a casserole to go along with the main course at Thanksgiving and Christmas dinners.

2 large sweet potatoes (1 to 1¼ pounds)
⅔ cup sugar
4 tablespoons (½ stick) unsalted butter,
     at room temperature
2 large eggs
1 teaspoon vanilla extract
1 teaspoon baking powder
⅓ cup milk
1 9-inch unbaked pie shell (see page 72)

In a pot of boiling water, cook the whole sweet potatoes until tender, about 40 minutes.

Preheat the oven to 350°F.

Peel the sweet potatoes and mash them completely in a large bowl. Add the sugar, butter, eggs, vanilla, and baking powder and mix thoroughly. Stir in the milk; the mixture will resemble a thick purée.

Pour the filling into the pie shell and set the pie on a baking sheet. Bake for 30 to 40 minutes, or until golden brown on top. Let the pie cool to room temperature before serving.

Serves 6

APRIL IN OHIO

M E N U

Pan-Fried Bluegill Fillets

Creamed Dried Corn

*Wilted Lettuce Salad
or
Red-Leaf Lettuce with
Sliced Eggs and Crumbled
Bacon*

Skillet Corn Bread

Rhubarb Pie

SUNDAY FISH FRY AT THE VAN HARLINGENS'

Lebanon, Ohio

Nothing gets a family together faster than a home-cooked Sunday dinner. The prospect of sitting down to such emotionally satisfying fare as Mother's cooking is too much for most people to resist. The Van Harlingen clan of Lebanon, Ohio, have turned the Sunday dinner into a family ritual.

By a cozy cabin on the verdant farmland for which the area is renowned, elm, honey oak, and ash trees offer a shady setting for the family's impromptu outings. A well-stocked pond provides an ample supply of bluegills for pan-frying.

The cabin is located on the 130-acre farm of Dr. George Van Harlingen— a physician who still makes house calls! —and his wife, Pat, who manages his medical office. In addition to their professional duties, the couple tend a rose garden, herb garden, two vegetable gardens, many flower gardens, and even a handful of cows and chickens. Somehow they also have time and energy to entertain family and friends on weekends.

I met the Van Harlingens through their daughter Vicky, who, as director of the Warren County Historical So-

ciety, invited me to give a talk on Country furnishings. I came to understand the specialness of this family's dinners together when I was asked to an outing in the country. "My brother, George, and my sister, Christine, and her family and I all have Sunday dinner with Mom and Dad at least twice a month," Vicky says. "The urge to get down to the cabin is especially strong in the spring. After months of winter weather, it's not unusual for us to pack

A pond stocked with bluegill (above) provides the main course for a family's rite-of-spring outing. The log cabin (left) was hand built by George Van Harlingen, who is about to join his wife, Pat, holding dog, and daughter, Vicky, at the table.

up at a moment's notice on a sunny day and head for that special place."

The cabin was built ten years ago by Dr. Van Harlingen and George, Jr., out of materials that had been assembled from the surrounding countryside over two decades—logs, floorboards salvaged from other buildings, and native fieldstone for the fireplace. "We cook and bake in the fireplace year-round, and get warm by it during ice-skating parties in winter," says Vicky.

In the spring and summer, the Sunday feasts are enjoyed outdoors around a trestle table that Vicky's father fashioned out of an 1810 walnut door. Flowering lilacs, native beauty bushes, snowballs, and cardinal bushes provide for lush bouquets.

Most of the family's favorite recipes, like creamed dried corn and wilted lettuce salad, which mother Pat prepares from memory, are actually in the German and Pennsylvania Dutch traditions handed down through father George's side of the family. "My father's father was the cook in his house," notes Vicky. "As the youngest son, he ended up taking care of a sickly mother, cooking and caring for her until she died, and didn't marry until he was thirty-six."

Situated halfway between the bustling cities of Dayton and Cincinnati, Lebanon has a population of about 10,000. First settled in the late eighteenth and early nineteenth centuries, it has retained its solid small-town values, thanks in large part to families like the Van Harlingens.

PAN-FRIED BLUEGILL FILLETS

If you look out the window of the airplane as you fly over the Midwest, you notice that the countryside is dotted with farm ponds and lakes. This is a conservation practice that is subsidized by the government. The lakes usually are stocked with bluegills and bass—the bluegills very small but much sweeter and superior in flavor to the bass.

Bluegill fillets (figure on using 5 to 6 per person; they're very small), or lake perch
All-purpose flour
Yellow cornmeal
Salt and freshly ground black pepper
Vegetable oil

Dredge the fish fillets in equal parts of flour and cornmeal and season them with salt and pepper.

Pour about 1½ inches of oil into a skillet and put it over moderately high heat. When the oil begins to shimmer, pan-fry the fillets quickly in the hot oil, until they are golden brown on both sides, about 5 to 8 minutes. The timing will depend on the size of the fish.

In a picnic setting, the dining room table moves outdoors with style, topped by a checkered cloth, pewter mugs and plates, and a ceramic butter receptacle shaped like a cow.

CREAMED DRIED CORN

George Van Harlingen's family came to Ohio from Pennsylvania and brought this recipe for dried corn with them. Dried corn is available in many supermarkets or can be ordered by mail (see Ohio listing, page 220, in Directory). To make it yourself for use throughout the year, preheat the oven to 140°F. Cook fresh ears of sweet corn in boiling water for 5 minutes. Drain and cut the kernels from the cobs. Spread the corn out in a single layer on baking sheets and bake, stirring from time to time, until very dry, 12 hours to 3 days, depending on the size of the corn and the humidity. Store in a muslin bag in a cool place or freeze indefinitely.

1 cup dried corn

2 tablespoons unsalted butter

½ cup heavy cream

Salt and freshly ground black pepper

Put the dried corn in a deep saucepan and add water to cover by about 1 inch. Set aside to soak overnight.

Next day, gently cook the corn in its soaking water over low heat for about 2 hours, or until it is puffed and soft; the corn will be creamy and thick. Add additional water, if necessary, to ensure that the corn does not dry out.

Stir in the butter and heavy cream and cook until thick. Season with salt and pepper to taste and serve hot.

Serves 4 to 6

WILTED LETTUCE SALAD

Vicky's grandfather, William Van Harlingen, was always the official cook of this lettuce salad. Being a "picky eater," it was the only salad he would eat.

1 large head leaf lettuce

6 lean bacon slices

1½ tablespoons cider vinegar

Salt and freshly ground black pepper

3 hard-cooked large eggs

Wash the lettuce and then spin-dry it. Tear the leaves into large bite-size pieces and set them aside.

In a large nonreactive skillet, fry the bacon until crisp. Remove the slices and drain them on paper towels; leave the bacon fat in the skillet.

Turn off the heat under the skillet and add the lettuce while the bacon fat is still hot. Toss to coat it well. Add the vinegar and season with salt and a generous amount of pepper. Slice the eggs thin and crumble the bacon and add them to the salad, tossing well until thoroughly combined. Serve warm.

Serves 4 to 6

Weathered wood bridge spans the Van Harlingen pond (above left). The lilacs of spring, available in profusion on the property (left), serve as a table decoration (right). The trestle table, attended by a blue-tick hound named Charlene and surrounded by garden-variety ladder-back chairs, was built out of a walnut-planked door used in the 1810s.

Corn, stone ground into meal at a nearby mill, guarantees the freshness of corn bread, cooked and served in a cast-iron skillet.

Skillet Corn Bread

1¼ cups yellow cornmeal

¾ cup all-purpose flour

2½ teaspoons baking powder

1 tablespoon sugar

½ teaspoon salt

2 large eggs

3 tablespoons unsalted butter, melted

1 cup milk

2 tablespoons unsalted butter

Preheat the oven to 425°F. Place a 9-inch cast-iron skillet in the oven and let it heat while you make the batter.

In a large bowl, combine the cornmeal, flour, baking powder, sugar, and salt.

In a small bowl, beat the eggs with the melted butter and milk until well blended.

Add the egg mixture to the dry ingredients and stir just until combined.

Drop the 2 tablespoons of butter into the heated skillet and swirl it around until the butter has completely melted. Pour in the batter and bake for 25 minutes, or until golden on top and crusty on the bottom. Cut into wedges and serve directly from the skillet.

Serves 6 to 8

For thirty years, Pat Van Harlingen's rhubarb pie (right) has been deliciously announcing the arrival of spring, as much a sign as the first dandelions and violets (left).

RHUBARB PIE

Pat Van Harlingen has been making this wonderful rhubarb pie for thirty years. The pie pastry is flawless—it always works perfectly.

PIE PASTRY

2¼ cups sifted all-purpose flour

2 teaspoons salt

¾ cup vegetable shortening

Sugar for sprinkling

FILLING

3 cups diced fresh spring rhubarb

1½ cups sugar

¼ cup all-purpose flour

Preheat the oven to 425°F. Make the pastry: Combine the flour and salt in a large bowl. Remove ⅓ cup of the mixture to a small bowl and set the large bowl aside.

Add ½ cup cold water to the small bowl and stir well to make a paste. Set aside.

To the large bowl, add the shortening and cut it into the flour using a pastry blender or two knives until the mixture resembles coarse meal. Add the paste and stir with a fork until the dough pulls together enough to form a ball. Divide the dough in half. Wrap one piece in plastic wrap and refrigerate it.

On a lightly floured surface, roll out the remaining piece of dough to about a ⅛-inch thickness. Fit the dough into a 9-inch pie pan and set it aside.

Make the filling: In a bowl, combine the rhubarb, sugar, and flour. Toss well to coat the rhubarb with the sugar and flour. Turn the rhubarb into the pie-crust.

Roll out the remaining dough and place it over the rhubarb filling. Trim the edges and crimp them decoratively. Cut 4 or 5 small slits in the top crust to make steam vents. Sprinkle the top of the pie with sugar.

Place the pie on a baking sheet and bake for 20 minutes. Lower the oven temperature to 350°F. and bake for 25 minutes more, or until the crust is golden brown. Serve warm or at room temperature.

Serves 6 to 8

MENU

Scalloped Potatoes and Ham

Asparagus Vinaigrette Salad

Butter-Crust Beer Bread

Chocolate Chip Melt Pie

Wine or Beer

Coffee

Springboro, Ohio

Sue Ellen Johnson introduced me to antiquing in the Ohio River Valley one sunny fall day, and I soon discovered that this activity rivals Big Eight Football as the number one regional pastime. Sue Ellen took me through dozens of shops along the highways and byways between her native Dayton and New Lebanon. All of them seemed to be full of knowledgeable browsers and buyers.

This is an area where the Colonial spirit is as much a part of tradition as it is in our earliest cities along the eastern seaboard; after all, it is America's original dumping ground—where pioneers emptied their wagons of cumbersome possessions before heading West. And Colonial custom carries over to the household, where entertaining centers around the Great Room, and its walk-in hearth that warms the spirits of visitors as it has for centuries.

Over the fireplace hang bunches of dried herbs, the product of a summer garden; strings of chile peppers and garlic; antique cookware and implements; and even an old cast-iron pot for cooking wintry soups and stews in the enormous hearth. "One of our fa-

vorite ways to spend an evening is to invite one or two other couples over for dinner in front of the fire," says Sue Ellen. Husband Steve, a builder specializing in authentic reproduction houses, designed and built theirs.

Modeled after an eighteenth-century Connecticut River Valley house, their home comes complete with a tavern. The tavern's wooden dowel gate dates back to a time when "opening up the bar" literally meant removing the padlock and raising the iron bar gate behind which the liquor was secured.

Entertaining comes naturally to Sue

Spring brings warm days to the Ohio River Valley, where Sue Ellen and Steve Johnson have their 18th-century reproduction home (above), but the nights are cold enough for a fire in the tavern room (left). A stretcher-base table from the 1750s is set for an intimate evening meal. The banister-back chairs have flame-stitch cushions; raised dowels on the bar signify "open for business."

Breakfast counter adjoins the Johnson kitchen, which is full of antique baskets still in use for transporting flowers, herbs, and food to and from the garden and houses of friends.

Ellen. Her mother cooked not just for five children, but for an unbroken stream of guests at the dinner table, and Sue Ellen was always helping out. Her grandmother's pink Spode china is frequently brought to her table, as is her collection of antique pewter plates.

For those special fireside gatherings, Sue Ellen favors hearty stews and soups or her favorite potato and ham casserole, American originals that she freely adapts to her family's tastes. The best of all times, however, may just well be when the fireplace is reserved for Steve and Sue Ellen, for that rare evening when they are left alone to enjoy a quiet supper for two.

SCALLOPED POTATOES AND HAM

4 large potatoes, peeled and parboiled
1 large onion, thinly sliced
1 to 2 pounds thick-sliced ham steaks
6 tablespoons (¾ stick) unsalted butter
¼ cup plus 2 tablespoons all-purpose flour
3 cups milk
3 cups shredded Cheddar cheese
2 teaspoons powdered mustard
1½ teaspoons Worcestershire sauce
1½ tablespoons dry sherry or dry vermouth
Salt and freshly ground black pepper

Preheat the oven to 350°F.

Slice the potatoes medium-thin. Separate the onion slices into rings. Cut the ham into large chunks. Layer the potatoes, onions, and ham in a large casserole.

In a heavy saucepan, melt the butter over moderate heat. Add the flour and cook, stirring constantly, until the mixture is smooth and bubbly. Remove from the heat and stir in the milk. Return to moderate heat and bring to a boil, whisking constantly. Cook over moderate heat for 3 minutes, whisking all the time.

One cup at a time, add the cheese and stir well until it has melted. Add the mustard, Worcestershire sauce, and sherry and season with salt and pepper to taste.

Pour the sauce over the potatoes, onions, and ham and bake for 45 to 60 minutes, or until the potatoes are cooked through and the top is browned.

Serves 4

ASPARAGUS VINAIGRETTE SALAD

If you are preparing this salad ahead of time, place the asparagus in the vinaigrette and seal in a lockable plastic bag to chill.

SALAD

1 large head Boston lettuce
1 pound fresh asparagus spears, steamed and chilled
1 hard-cooked large egg, sliced
2 thin slices red onion, separated into rings
Crumbled blue cheese

VINAIGRETTE

3 tablespoons safflower oil
2 tablespoons olive oil
2 tablespoons red wine vinegar
1 garlic clove, minced
1 teaspoon Dijon mustard
1 teaspoon sugar
1 teaspoon salt
¼ teaspoon freshly ground black pepper

Make a bed of lettuce leaves over the salad plates and arrange the asparagus spears on the lettuce. Top with the egg slices and about 6 rings of red onion.

In a jar, combine the vinaigrette ingredients and shake well. Pour the vinaigrette over the salad and sprinkle with the crumbled blue cheese.

Serves 2 to 4

Table is set with antique pewter plates, mugs, and candlesticks (left), whose glow mesmerizes a pair of household pets (below). The casserole holds scalloped potatoes and ham, served with beer batter bread and an asparagus salad.

*Old saloon-style swinging
doors are used as the front gate.
Bull's-eye glass panes beneath
the crown of the door provide a
Georgian detail.*

BUTTER-CRUST BEER BREAD

If you're wary of bread baking, relax—this couldn't be simpler.

- 2 cups self-rising flour
- 3 tablespoons sugar
- 1 12-ounce can beer (do not use light beer)
- 4 tablespoons (½ stick) unsalted butter, melted

Preheat the oven to 350°F. Oil or butter a standard loaf pan.

In a bowl, combine the flour, sugar, and beer and mix with a wooden spoon until well blended and sticky, about 1 minute.

Pour the dough into the prepared pan and bake for 30 minutes.

Remove the bread from the oven and pour the melted butter over the top. Bake for 30 minutes more, until lightly browned on top.

Cool in the pan, then remove, and serve with whipped butter.

Makes 1 loaf

CHOCOLATE CHIP MELT PIE

Jeremy and Jessica Johnson are fans of their mom's best-ever pie. It will bring out the chocolate-loving child in everyone.

- 1 cup semisweet chocolate chips
- ½ cup chopped walnuts or pecans
- 2 large eggs, beaten
- ½ cup firmly packed light brown sugar
- ½ cup granulated sugar
- 8 tablespoons (1 stick) unsalted butter, melted
- ½ cup all-purpose flour
- 1 teaspoon vanilla extract
- 1 9-inch unbaked pie shell (see page 72)
  Vanilla ice cream (optional)

Preheat the oven to 350°F.

In a large bowl, mix together the chocolate chips, nuts, and eggs. Add the sugars, butter, and flour. Stir in the vanilla.

Pour the filling into the pie shell and place the pie on a baking sheet.

Bake in the center of the oven for 30 minutes, or until the pastry is lightly browned and the filling is bubbling.

Serve warm or at room temperature, with vanilla ice cream, if desired.

Serves 6 to 8

Everybody's favorite cookie is adapted for dessert in this chocolate chip melt pie, which can be prepared the day before.

Dinner is served against a backdrop evoking the American frontier. The tiger-maple full-stock rifle, leather shot "powder purse," and collection of iron cooking utensils date from the 18th and early 19th centuries.

VERMONT FOR A SPRING SNOWFALL

Waitsfield, Vermont

COUNTRY KITCHEN
BREAKFAST AT JACKIE
AND BOB ROSE'S

A fanlight window marks the entrance to the converted Methodist Meeting House from the 1830s (above), which Jackie Rose now stocks with the freshest local products from the state of milk and honey. Assembled on a well-used butcher-block counter (right) are the ingredients for a Vermont breakfast; on the windowsill is an assortment of tin and ironstone molds.

When time is plentiful and the day stretches before you free of all tasks and obligations, breakfast becomes an opportunity for "doing things the long way," like squeezing oranges for juice, baking homemade "mapple" muffins, grilling thick slices of Canadian bacon, and whipping up fresh batter for a stack of buttermilk waffles.

Breakfast is served around an old French harvest table in the Vermont kitchen of Jackie and Bob Rose. This kitchen is the warm beating heart of the home where the Roses and their three children, now grown, have lived for over twenty-five years. With its brick floor, walk-in-size hearth, washed pine and painted furniture, and splendid views of the neighbor's Holstein dairy cows, it is a kitchen Norman Rockwell might have conjured up with his brush. The larder of Vermont Cheddars, maple syrups, and apple butters come from Jackie's in-town Country emporium, The Store. Both kitchen and store place great value on the wholesome bounty of the "state of milk and honey."

The meal is very much a traditional affair at the Roses', but at lunch and dinner, Jackie inclines toward a more experimental, and elegant, approach. "My mother couldn't boil water," she recalls with a laugh, "so I had to learn everything on my own." Newly married in the 1950s, she enrolled in a Cordon Bleu class taught by the legendary Dione Lucas at her apartment in the Dakota in New York City. "Dione was a pioneer in the field; one of her pupils was James Beard," notes Jackie. "Her class was like a romp through the pages of Escoffier. She thought modern time-saving conveniences like the blender were awful. We did everything the long way." Three decades later, Jackie still turns to her Lucas class notes for standard recipes—that is, when she's not adapting her own, such as buttermilk waffles made lighter with the addition of extra eggs.

Her fascination with the culinary arts led Jackie to open The Store twenty years ago, recently relocated to a converted Methodist meeting house of the 1830s in Waitsfield. Thirty-foot-long pine trusses span a 2,500-square-foot space chockablock with antiques, cookware, tabletop accessories, and a wide variety of native foods, such as sheep's

M E N U

Buttermilk Waffles

Thick-Cut Canadian Bacon

Butternut Muffins

"Mapple" Muffins

Vermont Sweet Corn Bread

*Condiments: Vermont
Harvest Cranapple Maple
Conserve, Apple Blueberry
Conserve, Cold Hollow
Apple Cider Jelly, and Cold
Hollow Apple Butter*

*Chilled Vermont
Apple Cider*

Coffee

milk cheese, apple cider jelly, and pickled fiddlehead ferns. "Sometimes I think of the business as my folly," Jackie confesses, "but I love cooking so much, it was just natural for me to go into it."

When she entertains at home, no detail in the presentation of food escapes Jackie. "My feeling is that if something looks good, it will taste good." Helping her own meals look good are English bone-handled flatware, originally her mother's, a collection of ironstone plates, brightly painted pottery cups from Chile, and a hand-carved wood cutting board.

This area of Vermont has increased in population and otherwise changed tremendously in thirty years, but like most settlers who were attracted here originally by the natural beauty of the land, the Roses still swear by the old values and traditions, such as using what is locally produced and grown to its fullest potential. "Living in Vermont, I base my menus on freshness and availability," says Jackie. But ever the inventive cook, what she can't buy, she'll grow. "In the summer, I have a garden that I plant with things I can't get up here, like Japanese greens. Last year, I planted French greens, but I got the seeds all mixed up and all summer long we didn't know which greens we were eating!"

◇◇◇◇◇◇

BUTTERMILK WAFFLES

Don't forget to put Vermont maple syrup on top to keep these waffles authentic.

> 6 **large eggs, separated and at room temperature**
> 12 **tablespoons (1½ sticks) unsalted butter, melted**
> 2 **cups buttermilk**
> 1 **teaspoon vanilla extract**
> 2 **cups all-purpose flour**
> **Pinch of salt**
> 2 **tablespoons sugar (optional)**
> **Butter for serving**
> **Vermont maple syrup for serving**

In a bowl, beat the egg whites until very stiff peaks form.

Using a food processor, combine the egg yolks, melted butter, buttermilk, and vanilla. Process for 6 seconds. Add the flour, salt, and sugar and turn the machine on and off four or five times, until blended. Scrape down the sides of the bowl.

Add the egg whites and turn the machine on and off two or three times, just to mix. Scrape down the sides of the bowl.

Cook the waffles in a waffle iron, following the manufacturer's directions. Serve hot, with butter and maple syrup.

Makes 6 to 8 waffles

◇◇◇◇◇◇

Whipped egg whites are the secret to the lighter-than-air waffles on the table (below). The English breadboard and knife handle were shaped by a talented wood-carver; the corn bread, by an antique mold. Country muffins fill a tartan-lined basket (right).

BUTTERNUT MUFFINS

1½ cups plus 1 tablespoon all-purpose
    flour
¾ cup unprocessed bran
1 tablespoon baking powder
½ teaspoon salt
1 cup packed granulated maple sugar or
    dark brown sugar
8 tablespoons (1 stick) unsalted butter,
    softened
1 cup milk
1½ teaspoons vanilla extract
2 large eggs
1 cup chopped butternuts or walnuts

Preheat the oven to 350°F. Grease one or two standard-size muffin tins and set aside.

In a large bowl, combine 1½ cups flour, bran, baking powder, salt, and sugar. Add the butter, milk, vanilla, and eggs and beat on high speed for about 3 minutes, until smooth. Scrape down the bowl from time to time if needed.

Lightly toss the nuts in 1 tablespoon flour to coat them lightly and prevent them from sinking to the bottom while baking. Fold the nuts into the batter.

Divide the batter among the prepared muffin cups and bake for 25 to 30 minutes, or until the muffins are cooked through and lightly browned.

Makes about 16 muffins

"MAPPLE" MUFFINS

Maple and apples combine here to make a tasty breakfast muffin.

1 cup all-purpose flour
1 cup whole wheat flour
½ teaspoon salt
1 cup milk
⅓ cup maple syrup
¼ cup vegetable oil
1 large egg
1 cup grated peeled apples

Preheat the oven to 400°F. Oil a 12-cup muffin tin.

In a bowl or on a sheet of wax paper, combine the flours and salt.

In a large bowl, combine the milk, maple syrup, oil, egg, and grated apple. Add the dry ingredients and stir with a wooden spoon just until blended. The mixture will be lumpy; do not overmix.

Spoon the batter into the prepared muffin cups and bake for 20 to 25 minues, or until the muffins are lightly browned.

Makes 1 dozen

VERMONT SWEET CORN BREAD

1 cup yellow cornmeal
1 cup all-purpose flour
½ cup granulated maple sugar
1 tablespoon plus 1 teaspoon baking
    powder
4 tablespoons unsalted butter, softened
1 cup milk
1 large egg
    Pinch of salt
    Powdered confectioners' or maple
        sugar for the top of the baked bread

Preheat the oven to 375°F. if using a deep cake mold or preheat to 425°F. if using an 8-inch square pan. Grease the mold or pan well and set it aside.

In a food processor, combine the cornmeal, flour, granulated sugar, baking powder, and butter. Turn the machine on and off a few times until the mixture becomes mealy. Add the milk and egg and process for 30 seconds, or until well mixed.

Turn the batter into the prepared pan and bake until a cake tester inserted in the center comes out clean, 40 to 50 minutes for the deep fancy mold or 25 to 30 minutes for the square pan. Cool the bread on a wire rack and sprinkle with the powdered sugar before serving.

Serves 6

JUNE IN VIRGINIA AND MARYLAND

Arlington, Virginia

Nancy Clark Reynolds is my idea of the ultimate hostess. She is undaunted by such out-of-the-ordinary events as entertaining the President of the United States in her home. Affectionately known by the Reagans, her longtime friends, as "the other Nancy," she arranged their welcome-back-to-Washington party and decided on a rather unconventional Mexican buffet for the occasion. "I love to do the unexpected," Nancy explains, by inviting a lively mix of people, serving interesting food, and entertaining in her genuine log cabin in suburban Arlington, Virginia, only minutes from the White House.

"The best thing about parties in my cabin is that protocol is thrown out the window," she says. Even when it's an elegant party for two hundred under a tent or a rip-roaring barbecue like the one she hosted for me when *American Country West* was published, Nancy creates a wonderful sense of informality that makes everyone on the guest list feel right at home. Filled with mementos from Nancy's

In western gear, Nancy Clark Reynolds awaits her guests by a life-size stag carved of wood.

years growing up on the family's ranch in Idaho, the cabin is a natural icebreaker. So are the sheep wagon from her native Salmon Mountains that's parked in the backyard and the life-size carved deer that stands at the front door. The deer is actually my contribution to the rustic atmosphere. I had strapped it to the top of my jeep when I was bringing it to Nancy and was stopped by a policeman who wanted to give me a summons for shooting game out of season!

As the daughter of former Senator D. Worth Clark of Idaho, and now a Washington, D.C., lobbyist in her own right, Nancy knows the do's and don'ts of high-level entertaining. "The easier the better" best sums up her formula for staging successful events. "After raising four children and becoming involved with a career full time, I realized that cooking no longer had the great appeal it once did for me. I could not entertain today the way I do without the help of Design Cuisine," the Washington catering firm with which she has had a long and happy relationship. "They know me, my kitchen, the layout of my house and yard, and what

MENU

Apple Fritters

Scallion Dip

*Tiny Corn Cups with
Venison Chili and
Scrambled Eggs*

Spring Lamb and Marinade

Chorizo Sausages

Sheepherder's Potatoes

*Vegetable Salad with
Lemon-Basil Vinaigrette*

*Green Bean, Garbanzo
Bean, and Red Bell Pepper
Salad*

Wild Rice Salad

*Cheddar and Emmenthaler
Cheese Sticks*

Seven-Grain Bread

Fresh Fruit Salad

Ice Cream Cones

Brownies

*Nancy's log cabin (left) resembles
a wilderness retreat, but is
actually only a short distance
from the White House, making it
an ideal setting for entertaining
the Capitol Hill set. When
Paul and Carol Laxalt
hosted a Basque-style barbecue
(above), the crowd was
standing-room only.*

I'm trying to do for my guests. I trust them completely."

Nancy's adaptable cabin became the perfect setting for friend Carol Laxalt's plans to host an informal political fundraiser, drawing on the colorful Basque heritage of her husband, former Senator Paul Laxalt of Nevada.

Carol arranged for a fresh lamb to be flown in from Nevada for roasting on the spit, supplied the waiters with the distinctive red berets and white shirts of the Basque country, and used authentic cesta (the wicker baskets familiar to jai alai fans) as centerpieces for the tables. She also provided the caterer with Papa Laxalt's Basque recipes. And she pulled up Nancy's Idaho covered wagon as a reminder of the sheep wagons used to settle the West.

As with the Laxalt party, one of the hallmarks of Nancy's get-togethers are the carefully thought-out themes reflected in the centerpieces and the seating plans that she and the caterer make up. "Place cards are a must," she says, "otherwise guests only sit with people they already know and many new friendships would not be formed. I also like to make sure each table has at least one solid conversationalist—someone who can be trusted to keep things moving along."

Tables decked out in traditional Basque colors and a sheep wagon of the type once used by ranchers in the Pyrenees (above right) carry out the theme of the party. A surprising turn on a Country favorite: fritters flavored with apple, nutmeg, and cheese (right).

APPLE FRITTERS

The slightly sweet flavor of fried apple fritters blends wonderfully with the tanginess of sour cream and scallions.

- ¼ **pound unsalted butter, cut into bits**
- ¼ **teaspoon freshly grated nutmeg**
- ¼ **teaspoon salt**
- ¾ **cup bread flour**
- 3 **eggs**
- ½ **cup grated Swiss cheese**
- ¼ **cup freshly grated Parmesan cheese**
- 1 **cup dried apple**
  Vegetable oil for deep frying

In a heavy medium saucepan, bring the butter, nutmeg, salt, and ¾ cup water to a boil over high heat. Off the heat, add the flour all at once and stir quickly to blend well.

Return to moderate heat and cook, stirring, constantly, until the mixture pulls away from the sides of the pan and becomes a soft mass, about 3 to 5 minutes.

Scrape the mixture into the bowl of

an electric mixer. One at a time, add the eggs, beating until each is completely absorbed before adding the next.

Fold in the cheeses until well distributed. Stir in the dried apple.

In a deep fryer or deep saucepan, heat several inches of oil to 350°. Working in batches, drop the batter by teaspoonfuls into the hot fat and deep fry until golden brown. Drain on paper towels, and serve with Scallion Dip.

Makes about 4 dozen

SCALLION DIP

- 2 **cups sour cream**
- ⅓ **cup minced scallions**

Combine well and divide into small bowls for serving.

Makes about 2½ cups

TINY CORN CUPS WITH VENISON CHILI AND SCRAMBLED EGGS

Corn cups make for unusually tidy finger food. Double the recipe for larger crowds, or serve the fillings on their own.

CORN CUPS

¼ pound unsalted butter, at room
   temperature
4 ounces cream cheese, at room
   temperature
1 cup all-purpose flour
1 cup minus 2 tablespoons yellow
   cornmeal
   Pinch of salt

Preheat the oven to 375°.

In a bowl, cream the butter and cream cheese until well blended. Add flour and mix well. Add cornmeal and salt and mix until smooth. Shape the dough into a disc.

On a lightly floured surface, roll out the cornmeal dough about ¼ inch thick. Use a biscuit cutter or the rim of a glass to cut out 30 2½ to 3-inch rounds of dough.

Place the circles into a mini-muffin mold and press them into a cup shape. Bake for 10 to 12 minutes, until golden.

Makes 2½ dozen

VENISON CHILI

3 tablespoons bacon drippings or butter
½ cup minced onion
½ garlic clove, minced
1½ pounds ground venison
1¼ cups chopped tomatoes
¾ teaspoon salt
½ bay leaf
1 teaspoon sugar
¼ cup dry red wine
2 teaspoons to 2 tablespoons chili
   powder (to taste)

*Bite-size corn cups offer
tastings of venison chili and a
pepper-egg filling.*

In a large saucepan, melt bacon drippings over moderate heat. Add onion and garlic and cook until fragrant.

Add venison and sauté until just browned. Stir in tomatoes, salt, bay leaf, sugar, red wine, and chili powder until well mixed. Reduce the heat to low, cover and simmer for about 1 hour, until thick and tasty.

Spoon a dollop of chili atop the eggs before serving.

Makes enough filling for about 5 dozen corn cups

SCRAMBLED EGGS

4 tablespoons unsalted butter
1 tablespoon minced shallots
2 tablespoons chopped red bell pepper
2 tablespoons chopped green bell pepper
1 tablespoon minced scallions
1 teaspoon minced jalapeño pepper (or
   more to taste)
5 eggs
2 tablespoons heavy cream
   Salt and freshly ground pepper

In a large skillet, melt the butter over moderate heat. Add the shallots, bell peppers, scallions, and jalapeño and sauté until soft, about 4 minutes.

In a bowl, beat the eggs with the cream. Pour the egg mixture over the peppers and scramble them, stirring as they begin to set. Season with salt and pepper to taste.

Spoon a bit of the egg mixture into each corn cup and top with chili.

Makes enough filling for about 5 dozen corn cups

SPRING LAMB AND MARINADE

The marinade can be halved and quartered, but this recipe will yield enough to marinate a 35-pound lamb. You'll need a lot of refrigerator space to hold it.

> 1 whole lamb, dressed
> Olive oil
> 20 garlic cloves, crushed
> ½ cup coarsely ground black pepper
> ¼ cup fresh rosemary, crumbled
> ¼ cup fresh thyme
> 2 tablespoons salt
> 10 bay leaves
> 1 cup fresh lemon juice or red wine

Combine all the marinade ingredients. Roll whole lamb in marinade and refrigerate overnight, turning frequently.

Grill over mesquite wood on a spit until done. (See page 100 for preparation of mesquite barbecue pit.) Lamb should be served medium-rare.

SHEEPHERDER'S POTATOES

This update of a traditional Basque dish, from a Laxalt family recipe, goes especially well with lamb.

> 5 medium potatoes, cut into ¼-inch slices
> 1 medium onion, very thinly sliced
> ¼ pound bacon, cooked and crumbled
> Salt and freshly ground black pepper
> 1 quart chicken stock
> ¼ cup freshly grated Romano cheese
> ¼ cup freshly grated Parmesan cheese
> ½ cup shredded Emmenthaler cheese

Preheat the oven to 350°F.

In a large, well-buttered, ovenproof casserole, alternately layer potatoes, onion, and bacon. Season with salt and pepper. Pour chicken stock over potatoes and onion to fill three-quarters of the casserole.

Bake for 1 hour, or until potatoes are tender. Remove from oven and sprinkle with the cheeses. Return to oven and bake until golden brown and crusty.

Serves 8 to 10

Paul and Carol Laxalt (left) offer up a batch of chorizo, a spicy Spanish sausage, which has been grilled over a mesquite-stoked fire used to roast the lamb. Attractive spatterware plate (right) holds meats, salads, and bread—the bounty of the feast.

VEGETABLE SALAD WITH LEMON-BASIL VINAIGRETTE

VEGETABLES

> 12 small asparagus tips
> 1 small head broccoli, cut into florets
> 12 orange baby carrots
> 6 ounces fresh green beans
> 12 yellow plum tomatoes

VINAIGRETTE

> ¾ cup tightly packed fresh basil leaves
> 3 large shallots
> 2 tablespoons white wine vinegar
> Juice of 2 large lemons
> ¼ teaspoon sugar
> ¾ cup vegetable oil
> ¾ cup olive oil
> Salt and freshly ground pepper

Blanch each vegetable, except the tomatoes, separately, and cool under cold running water. Trim the asparagus, broccoli, carrots, and beans. Keep crisp in separate bowls of ice water.

In a food processor, combine the basil and shallots and process until minced. Add the vinegar, lemon juice, and sugar and process for 10 seconds. With the processor running, add the vegetable and olive oils in a thin stream and process until emulsified. Season to taste with salt and pepper.

About 15 minutes before serving, drain the vegetables and thoroughly pat dry. Arrange them over a serving plate and drizzle on some of the lemon-basil vinaigrette.

Serves 8 to 12; vinaigrette makes about 2 cups

To complement the Basque menu, a guitarist (above) strums native folk music. The three-vegetable salad, in traditional Basque colors of red, white, and green, and the potato-cheese casserole (right) are hearty accompaniments to grilled meat.

GREEN BEAN, GARBANZO BEAN, AND RED BELL PEPPER SALAD

The colorful bean salad is simple to prepare.

3 pounds fresh green beans, trimmed and steamed until crisp-tender

1 can (16 ounces) garbanzo beans, drained

2 red bell peppers, seeded and diced

1 cup tomato-basil vinaigrette (see page 40 and add ¼ cup chopped tomatoes to Lemon-Basil Vinaigrette recipe)

Combine green beans, garbanzo beans, and red peppers. Toss with vinaigrette to taste.

Serves 8 to 10

WILD RICE SALAD

Currants and dry sherry give this salad a special sweetness and zest.

1 cup dried currants

½ cup dry sherry

1 cup wild rice

4⅔ cups chicken stock, boiling

6 tablespoons (¾ stick) unsalted butter

1 cup brown rice

1 cup slivered almonds

½ cup chopped fresh parsley

Salt and freshly ground pepper

In a small saucepan, bring the currants and sherry to a boil. Reduce heat and simmer for 5 minutes. Set aside.

Place the wild rice, 2 cups of the boiling stock, and 2 tablespoons of the

Confetti salad mixture of brown and wild rice is garnished with slivers of peppers and placed near a reminder of the West.

butter in the top of a double boiler over simmering water. Cook, covered, for 1 hour.

Meanwhile, place the brown rice, the remaining 2⅔ cups boiling stock, and 2 tablespoons of the butter in a medium saucepan. Bring to a boil, reduce heat to low, and cook until all the water is absorbed, about 50 minutes.

In a small skillet, sauté the almonds in the remaining 2 tablespoons butter over low heat until lightly toasted.

Combine the wild rice, brown rice, currants with sherry, almonds, and parsley in a large mixing bowl. Season to taste with salt and pepper and toss.

Place in a decorative bowl and serve immediately.

Serves 8 to 10

BROWNIES

Fudgy, chocolaty brownies are an American staple —perfect for dessert or snacks.

4 tablespoons unsalted butter

4 ounces unsweetened chocolate

4 eggs at room temperature

¼ teaspoon salt

1 to 2 cups sugar

1 teaspoon vanilla extract

1 cup sifted all-purpose flour

1 cup chopped pecans

Preheat the oven to 350°F. Butter a 9 x 13-inch baking pan. In a saucepan, melt the butter with the chocolate over low heat just until melted. Set aside to cool to room temperature.

In a mixing bowl, beat the eggs with the salt until foamy. Add the sugar and vanilla and beat until the sugar dissolves. Stir in the melted chocolate and butter mixture and mix well. Fold in the flour and pecans.

Turn the brownie batter into the prepared pan and smooth the top. Bake for 22 to 25 minutes, until a toothpick comes out almost clean. Let cool on a rack before cutting into 1-inch squares.

Makes about 4 dozen

An all-American finale to the international feast is a plateful of chocolate-iced brownies.

F Blue Ridge Mountains, Virginia

riendly is what our life on the back porch is all about here," says Cornelia Wickens of her family's weekends at their 1890 country home in the Blue Ridge Mountains of Virginia. In their hideaway hamlet, she, husband Bill, and two small children find the peaceful life-style that usually eludes them during busy weekdays in Washington, D.C., where Corrie runs with her partner, Larry Hicks, one of my favorite Country emporiums, The American Store.

"In some small towns," Corrie explains, "you have to make plans to get together with friends, just as in a city. But when the street you live on is the entire village, as here, invitations to visit become less formal, exchanged while swapping vegetables or picking up the mail."

The back porch is the center of Corrie's entertaining in spring and summer, for it offers a magnificent view of the mountains and, in the foreground, colorful herb gardens, vegetable gardens, and some two hundred fruit trees which the Wickenses themselves have planted. Long luncheons and leisurely suppers take place here amid wicker rockers and cane chairs, all painted white, in a setting that evokes the genteel Victorian era. "I grew up fascinated by the period and was always studying family photos to see how my grandparents had lived," Corrie recalls. She continued the interest on an academic level, majoring in American Studies at college. Dressed in a long gingham jumper with a white lace blouse, Corrie remains the picture of a turn-of-the-century romantic.

Interestingly, there was no back

White wicker rockers and chairs and antique linens dress up a back porch (left) in romantic Victorian splendor. Flowers and herbs like the rosemary and sage garnishing the chicken dish all come from Corrie Wickens' garden (above), within view of the porch.

MENU

*Crudités and
Parsley-Chive Dip*

Chilled Tomato Soup

Country Garden Chicken

*Dilled Potato Salad with
Prosciutto and Blue Cheese*

*Minted Lemon and Lime
Cups*

Lemon-Nut Tea Cakes

Spicy Mint Tea

porch on the house when the Wickenses acquired it. Like most residences in the town, the house had a front porch, but it had scarcely a window from which to enjoy the views in the back. "It was typical of the era for a house to face the street," she says, "but we knew the best views were from the back." Corrie was not so doggedly Victorian as to ignore the scenic potential, and they built a sweeping new porch in the same style as the front, even duplicating the original gingerbread trim. "It's on the back porch that we really live much of the time today."

A decade from now, when Bill's orchard of nectarines, plums, apples, and peaches has reached maturity, it will be from Corrie's beloved back porch that the family will enjoy the spectacle of their blossoms and their fruit.

PARSLEY-CHIVE DIP

¾ cup mayonnaise

¾ cup sour cream

⅓ cup minced fresh parsley

3 tablespoons freshly snipped chives

1 crushed garlic clove

1 tablespoon wine vinegar

⅛ teaspoon salt

¼ teaspoon pepper

Fresh dill sprigs for garnish

Mix ingredients together and refrigerate overnight. Garnish with dill, if desired, and serve with your favorite fresh vegetables.

CHILLED TOMATO SOUP

Make this when your garden is bursting with ripe red tomatoes.

1 medium cucumber, peeled, halved lengthwise, and seeded

1 medium onion, coarsely chopped

4 to 5 large fresh basil leaves

3 large very ripe tomatoes, peeled, seeded, and coarsely chopped, with juice reserved

1 tablespoon salt

1 teaspoon sugar

½ teaspoon freshly ground black pepper

2 cups canned tomato juice

1 cup sour cream

Fresh basil leaves for garnish

Coarsely chop the cucumber. In a food processor fitted with a metal blade, combine the cucumber, onion, and basil. Process until finely chopped.

Add the chopped tomatoes and their juice and process until puréed. Add the salt, sugar, pepper, and tomato juice and mix well.

Working in batches if necessary, add the sour cream and process until thoroughly mixed.

Pour the soup into a large bowl, cover, and refrigerate until chilled, 4 hours or more.

Serve in soup plates or bowls, garnished with fresh basil leaves.

Serves 6 to 8

An illustrated seed box from the early 1900s (far left) contains hors d'oeuvres of garden-fresh vegetables and an herbal dip served in a cabbageware bowl. Luncheon plates hand-painted with herb designs are the china of choice for a cook whose recipes like this basil-enhanced soup (left) are redolent with fresh herbs.

COUNTRY GARDEN CHICKEN

A Corrie creation, this dish produces chicken that is wonderfully juicy and tender.

4 whole chicken breasts with skin, split
   Salt and freshly ground black pepper
8 tablespoons (1 stick) unsalted butter
2 pounds fresh asparagus spears, or 2
      10-ounce packages frozen asparagus
      spears
1 tablespoon all-purpose flour
1 cup heavy cream, scalded
16 fresh sage leaves
16 fresh rosemary branches
¾ cup dry white wine
   Sage and rosemary sprigs for garnish

Preheat the oven to 350°F.

Season the chicken with salt and pepper. In a large skillet, melt 4 tablespoons of the butter over moderate heat. Add 4 chicken breast halves and brown on both sides. Remove with tongs and brown the remaining breast halves. Reserve the cooking liquid and arrange the chicken breasts in a single layer in a large shallow roasting pan.

Meanwhile, steam the asparagus until crisp-tender. Cut the spears into 2-inch lengths. In a food processor, chop the asparagus.

In a heavy nonreactive saucepan, melt the remaining 4 tablespoons of butter over moderate heat. Stir in the flour and cook, stirring, for 2 to 3 minutes without letting it color. Gradually add the cream and cook, stirring constantly, for 1 minute. Remove from the heat and stir in the chopped asparagus.

Tuck 2 fresh sage leaves under the skin of each chicken breast. Place the rosemary branches between the chicken breasts so they will add flavor while the chicken bakes.

Add the chicken cooking juices and wine to the asparagus sauce and pour over the chicken breasts. Cover the pan with aluminum foil and bake, basting with the sauce from time to time, for 40 minutes. Uncover and bake for 30 minutes more, or until the chicken is tender.

Transfer the chicken and sauce to a platter and discard the rosemary. Garnish with fresh rosemary and surround the chicken with a wreath of fresh sage.

Serves 4 to 8

The porch addition to the 1890s house, overlooking a sea of flowers, incorporates Victorian detailing such as the spindlework railing and lacy column brackets.

DILLED POTATO SALAD WITH PROSCIUTTO AND BLUE CHEESE

Each bite of the creamy dilled potato salad reveals another flavor.

2½ to 3 pounds small red new potatoes in their skins

2 tablespoons white wine vinegar

½ cup chopped fresh dill

½ cup chopped scallions (including some of the green parts)

1½ cups diced celery

1 cup sour cream

½ cup mayonnaise, preferably homemade

8 to 10 thin slices prosciutto ham, cut into bits

¼ to ½ cup crumbled blue cheese

In a large pot of salted boiling water, cook the potatoes until fork-tender. Drain and quarter the smallest potatoes. Cut the remainder into medium slices.

Put the potatoes in a large bowl and sprinkle with the vinegar while they are still warm.

In a bowl, combine the dill, scallions, celery, sour cream, mayonnaise, prosciutto, and blue cheese. Pour the dressing over the potatoes and toss to coat thoroughly.

Cover the potato salad and refrigerate until chilled, 3 to 4 hours.

Serves 8

LEMON-NUT TEA CAKES

1¾ cups all-purpose flour

½ cup sugar

2 teaspoons baking powder

¼ teaspoon salt

½ cup chopped almonds

1 teaspoon grated lemon rind

1 large egg, beaten

1 cup milk

4 tablespoons (½ stick) butter, melted

1 teaspoon vanilla extract

Preheat the oven to 400°F. Butter a 12-cup muffin tin or a heart-shaped baking pan.

In a bowl, combine the flour, sugar, baking powder, and salt. Stir in the almonds and lemon rind and mix well.

In another bowl, combine the egg, milk, and butter. Add the vanilla. Stir the liquid ingredients into the dry ingredients just until moistened.

Spoon the batter into the prepared muffin cups or baking pan and bake for 15 to 20 minutes, or until golden brown on top.

Serves 12

MINTED LEMON AND LIME CUPS

The hottest summer day is no challenge to these refreshing individual desserts. Save the lemon and lime pulp for a pitcher of homemade limeade.

4 large lemons

4 large limes

1 pint vanilla ice cream, softened

1 pint lemon or lime sherbet, softened

2 to 3 tablespoons green crème de menthe

Fresh mint leaves

Wash the lemons and limes. Cut off one side of each lemon or lime. Using a grapefruit knife or spoon, scoop out the pulp, leaving just the shell. If necessary, cut a thin slice off the opposite side of the fruit to make a flat bottom.

In a bowl, combine the ice cream and sherbet. Spoon the mixture into the hollowed-out lemon and lime cups and drizzle with crème de menthe.

Arrange the cups snugly in a metal dish or pan and freeze until firm.

Place the cups on a serving platter and garnish with mint leaves around their bases and on top of the ice cream. Serve at once.

Serves 8

Sage and a wreath of tarragon embellish the potato salad.

SPICY MINT TEA

10 fresh mint leaves

  1 teaspoon ground cloves

½ teaspoon ground allspice

½ teaspoon ground cinnamon

  6 tea bags

¾ cup fresh orange juice

  2 tablespoons fresh lemon juice

Bring about 2 quarts of water to a boil over high heat.

Meanwhile, in a large teapot or heat-proof bowl, combine the mint, cloves, allspice, and cinnamon. Add 6 cups of the boiling water and the tea bags. Cover and steep for 5 minutes.

Strain the tea and stir in the orange juice and lemon juice. Serve hot, as is, or dilute with 4 cups of cold water and serve over ice.

Serves 6

*Delicately painted ceramic basket
and scalloped dish hold tea cakes
and a frozen dessert served in
lemon and lime shells.*

Saint Michaels, Maryland

The folk Victorian porch of this Eastern Shore summer house (above) conveys a message as friendly as iced-down wedges of farm-fresh watermelon (above right).

In a Victorian farmhouse on the Eastern Shore of Maryland's Chesapeake Bay, entertaining is as easy as walking down to the dock and pulling in nets with the day's catch of succulent blue crabs, the local specialty. Here, the goal for entertaining is just as simple: to enjoy people.

Growing up in the nation's capital, I spent many a summer on the Eastern Shore and my fondest memories are of the rural back country, where local fish houses provided some of the best eating around. Whenever Marilyn and John Hannigan invite me to their getaway home on the bay, I can't wait to smell the salt air and taste the sweet crab.

Marilyn is the owner of a Washington, D.C., shop, Cherishables, which specializes in eighteenth- and nineteenth-century American furniture, quilts, and folk art, a business that keeps her on the go five days a week, and through which we became friends. John, an executive with the Rouse Company, is equally busy scouting new projects for the high-flying development firm that built Harborplace in Baltimore, Faneuil Hall in Boston, and South Street Seaport in New York. "With schedules like ours," Marilyn says, "we found we had little time for seeing friends, and one year of that experience was all we could take—we missed our friends tremendously."

Buying the bay house as a weekend retreat, no more than a two-hour drive from their Washington home, helped the Hannigans redress the problem. "The house has become a ready means for getting our favorite people together, without fuss or complications," observes Marilyn. Although she may invite as many as twelve or fifteen people for dinner, the guests themselves ease the load of preparing. "People arrive with potato salad or a pie and they love going shopping with me at one of the local farm markets for the pick of the fresh produce."

Informality is the rule. Tasks in the kitchen may be followed by a spirited game of volleyball or croquet, a marathon Trivial Pursuit match, or a long lazy walk through the rural countryside. "The place lulls you into getting the greatest pleasure and relaxation out of doing the most ordinary things," Marilyn says.

Cocktails are offered beginning at five o'clock out on the porch, facing the Bay. Crab boils are often served on

*Rustic dining at the shore means
a grassy carpet underfoot for
croquet players and fans, and
newspapers spread out as the
traditional tablecloth for a meal
of Maryland crabs.*

picnic tables covered with newspapers instead of fancy linens. "I like to do all the cooking myself," says Marilyn. "That's my style. I'm of the belief that if you are going to turn over the job to somebody else in the kitchen, then you might as well take your friends out to a restaurant."

She comes by cooking naturally: "I grew up digging into things in the kitchen, and my mother encouraged me. She always let me bake my own birthday cakes. When I was a small girl, they were simple layer cakes," she says, laughing, "but by the time I was a teen-ager, they had grown into major productions!"

Though well versed in the art of preparing gourmet fare, today Marilyn favors simple foods. "Why make the difficult meals when a simple meal like leg of lamb with a heap of crisp, oven-roasted new potatoes is guaranteed to be memorable?"

MRS. MURPHY'S DEVILED EGGS

Mrs. Murphy, a wonderful cook, is the mother of Marilyn's assistant at her shop in Washington.

9 hard-cooked eggs, cooled
3 tablespoons mayonnaise
2 teaspoons Dijon mustard
1½ teaspoons white wine vinegar
¾ teaspoon salt
½ teaspoon paprika
½ teaspoon minced fresh tarragon
¼ teaspoon Tabasco sauce

Remove the shells from the eggs; rinse the eggs and pat them dry with paper towels. Halve the eggs lengthwise and put the egg yolks in a small bowl. Set the cooked whites aside.

Mash the egg yolks lightly with a fork. Add all of the remaining ingredients and stir to combine thoroughly. Pipe or spoon the egg yolk mixture into the egg white halves, cover, and chill until serving time.

Serves 6

A mound of crabs to satisfy even the heartiest appetites (above left) can easily be caught in the crab pots sold at a local waterman's shack (below).

STEAMED CHESAPEAKE BAY BLUE CRABS

Everyone in the area cooks and eats Chesapeake Bay blue crabs the traditional way—steamed with Old Bay Seasoning and then cracked open with large wooden mallets. Large quantities of these crabs are shipped to fish markets around the country.

½ to ¾ cup Old Bay Seasoning
½ cup salt
3 cups distilled white vinegar
3 cups beer or water
About 36 live Maryland blue crabs, depending on size

Prepare a charcoal grill and burn the coals until red hot.

In a nonreactive bowl, combine the Old Bay Seasoning, salt, vinegar, and beer. Mix well.

Place a very large metal steaming pot with a tight-fitting cover on the grill and set the steaming rack in place. Arrange about half the crabs on the rack and pour half of the seasoning over the crabs. Add the remaining crabs and douse with the remaining seasoning mixture. Cover tightly and steam for 25 to 30 minutes, or until the crabs are bright red. Serve at once.

Serves 6

Chesapeake Bay blue crabs, steamed to the pink, require no plate or fancy condiments for serving; a sturdy mallet and mug of beer will do.

GRILLED CORN ON THE COB

6 large ears sweet corn with husks attached

¼ to ½ pound (1 to 2 sticks) unsalted butter, softened or melted

Pull the cornhusks back and remove the silk. Dip the corn in cold water and generously coat each ear with butter. Pull the husks back into place and cook the corn about 4 inches above the ash-covered charcoal. Turn the corn frequently until cooked through, 8 to 10 minutes.

Remove the husks and serve hot with additional butter.

Serves 6

BLACK BOTTOM CUPCAKES

Marilyn Hannigan prefers to make these cupcakes in miniature muffin tins with miniature muffin liners. They can be served at parties, where they'll be a boon to those who don't want a great deal of dessert but need to satisfy a sweet tooth.

FILLING

1 8-ounce package cream cheese, softened

⅓ cup sugar

⅛ teaspoon salt

1 large egg, beaten

1 cup semisweet chocolate chips

CUPCAKES

1½ cups all-purpose flour

1 cup sugar

¼ cup unsweetened cocoa powder

1 teaspoon baking soda

½ teaspoon salt

⅓ cup vegetable oil

1 tablespoon distilled white vinegar

1 teaspoon vanilla extract

Preheat the oven to 350°F. Have ready miniature or regular-size muffin tins and cupcake liners.

Prepare the filling: In a small bowl, cream the cream cheese with the sugar and salt. Add the egg and beat well. Stir in the chocolate chips and set aside.

Make the cupcakes: In a large bowl, sift together the flour, sugar, cocoa, baking soda, and salt. Add the oil, vinegar, vanilla, and 1 cup of water; beat well until thoroughly combined.

Spoon the cupcake batter into the cupcake liners, filling them about three-quarters full. Drop a small dollop of the filling mixture on top of each cupcake. Bake for 20 minutes and remove from the oven. Let cool on wire racks.

Makes about 40 miniature cupcakes or 18 regular-size cupcakes

On the Maryland shore, the summer standards of cupcakes (above) and corn (above left) receive special attention.

For dessert, china plates and a
bottle of Champagne (above)
restore elegance to the occasion of
a simple crab boil. When the
boats are in harbor (left), it's only
a short boardwalk from the house
to find out what the fishing and
crabbing is like.

LONG ISLAND SUMMERS

MENU

BUFFET IN THE BARN

Terry's Margaritas

Marinated Shrimp with Lemons and Onions

Crispy Fried Chicken Wings

Mustard and Apricot-Glazed Baked Ham

Fusilli Pasta Salad with Zucchini, Red Onion, Pine Nuts, and Walnut Pesto

Tomato, Red Onion, and Basil Salad with Mib's Vinaigrette

Hard Rolls

Bridgehampton Chardonnay

Kathleen's Devil's Food Cake

Open Bar

Bridgehampton, Long Island

I always love birthdays—anybody's birthday! Growing up, I felt cheated out of a real party because my birthday fell in July, when the school year was long over. My boyfriend Chris Mead really went all out for me one year when he invited ninety—count 'em, ninety—people to the summer house in Bridgehampton for a gala celebration under the stars by the swimming pool.

But there were no stars: The elements conspired against Chris, whose ingenuity came to the rescue. In fact, this party turned out to be one of the most successful we have ever hosted. (Even though it was a party for me, I couldn't stand by without helping.)

By noon of that day it was raining, and raining hard. Nothing else was going as planned either. The phone had to be taken off the hook (the guest list threatened to double with each call); the kids needed attention; a recipe

Dressed up for the occasion, the barn features a fancywork quilt, makeshift lace window curtains, and serving utensils, including an old wooden tray full of fried chicken wings.

wasn't working; and our house guests were bored because they couldn't go to the beach. Worst of all: We knew there was no way the modest house could contain a crowd as large as the pool and patio area could.

Luckily, it happens that on the property, next to the pool, stands a barn that Chris intended to convert into guest quarters. He had gotten as far as cleaning it up and whitewashing its walls, but that was all. As the storm continued, it dawned on us that the barn might be a suitable place to hold the party. The sole drawback was that it had no electricity. But then we imagined the space illuminated by scores of candles, and we managed to find an electrician (on Saturday!) to install two spotlights just before zero hour.

As it turned out, the barn provided a better setting for the party than the outdoor area. It was spacious enough for ninety guests, but it still had an intimacy that encouraged the crowd to mix and mingle. Food was set out at three stations to keep things flowing: Two round tables were heaped with pesto-flavored pasta salad and tomato, red onion, and basil salad, and a long rustic table offered buffet-style platters of marinated shrimp, my favorite crispy fried chicken wings, and baked ham. An old cupboard, with doors missing, became the bar. So we all could enjoy ourselves, Chris hired bartenders and waiters to keep the food moving and to clean up afterward—a real bonus if you've ever had to face up to the aftermath of a large party.

When the rain finally passed, a few fun-loving souls, including the photographer (Chris), decided to enjoy the pool, dress clothes and all. The loud splashes, along with the waterlogged film, pronounced the evening a success.

TERRY'S MARGARITAS

My brother Terry is a master of Margarita making. He takes his work seriously. "Being the maker means that you are the taster, and the taster has to decide which formula is the perfect formula. It's hard work, but somebody has to do it," he says.

Lime wedges
Salt
Ice
Fresh lime juice
Triple Sec
Tequila (preferably gold)

Use a wedge of lime to moisten the lip of a stemmed glass. Dip the moistened rim into salt to coat it. Set the glass aside. Fill a cocktail shaker or any large widemouthed jar with a tight-fitting lid with ice. Depending on how many Margaritas you want to make, and depending on how large you want them to be, pour equal parts of lime juice, Triple Sec, and tequila over the ice. Cover and shake briskly. Taste and adjust the flavor if necessary.

Strain the mixture into the prepared glass and serve at once.

Serves 1

Mary's brother, Terry Ellisor, whips up a batch of Margaritas. Fresh limes are the key ingredient according to South of the Border tradition.

MARINATED SHRIMP WITH LEMONS AND ONIONS

Emelie Tolley made these shrimp, which will be a hit at any party. Be sure you have enough to go around.

3 pounds medium shrimp, cooked and shelled
3 medium onions, thinly sliced
2 lemons, thinly sliced
1 cup chopped fresh parsley
Salt and freshly ground black pepper
½ teaspoon Tabasco sauce
Olive oil
3 bay leaves

In a glass or ceramic serving dish, layer the shrimp, onions, lemons, and parsley. Season generously with salt and pepper and sprinkle with the Tabasco. Pour on enough olive oil to cover. Tuck the bay leaves under the top layer.

Cover with plastic wrap and refrigerate for 6 to 8 hours, or until chilled and flavorful. Serve directly from the dish.

Serves 10 to 12

CRISPY FRIED CHICKEN WINGS

This recipe, suggested by a butcher at the local IGA store, is one of my favorites.

18 chicken wings
4 cups milk
2 cups all-purpose flour
2 teaspoons salt
2 teaspoons freshly ground black pepper
About 1 quart peanut or safflower oil

Divide each chicken wing at the joint into two parts. Put the wings in a bowl or shallow pan and cover with the milk. Cover and refrigerate overnight.

In a shallow dish, combine the flour and salt and pepper. Pour about 1 inch of oil into each of two deep, heavy skillets and set them over moderately high heat. While the oil heats, coat the wings with the flour mixture. When the surface of the oil begins to shimmer and is very hot, add the wings and fry on one side for 4 minutes. Do not crowd the wings.

Turn the wings and fry for 4 minutes more, or until they are very crispy. Continue coating and frying until all of the wings are cooked.

Drain well on paper towels and serve warm or at room temperature.

Serves 12

MUSTARD AND APRICOT-GLAZED BAKED HAM

Glazed baked ham, like this Emelie Tolley specialty, is as basic and as American as apple pie. Be sure to save the ham fat and bone for soups and casseroles.

1 precooked 10- to 12-pound bone-in ham
¼ cup whole cloves
1 cup Dijon mustard
1 cup apricot jam
2 cups dry white wine, beer, or ginger ale

Preheat the oven to 300°F. Trim away any excess fat from the ham, leaving a thin layer to keep the meat moist during baking. Using a sharp knife, score the ham to form a 1-inch diamond pattern on the surface. Insert a clove at the intersections of the lines.

Place the ham, fat side up, in a shallow baking pan. Spread a generous layer of mustard over the top of the ham, covering it completely; take care not to dislodge the cloves. Spread a layer of jam over the mustard. Pour the wine into the bottom of the pan, around the ham.

Bake the ham, basting frequently with the pan juices, for 1 to 1½ hours, or until the internal temperature registers 140°F. on a meat thermometer.

Set the ham aside for at least 10 minutes before slicing it. Serve hot or at room temperature.

Serves 14 to 16

CHRIS MEAD

Beverly Jacomini and helper (top left). Sandy and John Horvitz (top right). From left to right: Ninky Savage, Stan Freeman, Sue Eden, and Pete Savage (above left). Katrin Tolleson and Michael Skott (above right).

Baskets hold the basics while crowd-size pottery contains the tomato salad and the fusilli dressed in walnut pesto (above). Among the festive birthday scenes preserved on film that fell into the pool along with the photographer: Chris Mead brings in the cake and Mary prepares to blow out the candles (right).

FUSILLI PASTA SALAD WITH ZUCCHINI, RED ONION, PINE NUTS, AND WALNUT PESTO

My friend Mary Higgins is responsible for this recipe. The salad can be made well ahead of time (it keeps for days) and actually tastes even better after the pesto has a chance to "mature."

WALNUT PESTO

    3 cups firmly packed fresh basil leaves
    8 sprigs Italian flat-leaf parsley
    3 large garlic cloves
 1½ teaspoons salt
    3 tablespoons pine nuts
   ½ cup walnut pieces
   ¾ cup olive oil
   ¾ cup freshly grated Parmesan cheese
    Freshly ground black pepper

PASTA SALAD

 1½ pounds fusilli (corkscrew) pasta
  4 to 5 medium zucchini, cut into
      medium julienne
   2 large red onions, chopped
    Salt and freshly ground black pepper

Prepare the pesto: Using a food processor fitted with a metal blade, combine the basil, parsley, garlic, and salt. Process until finely minced. Add the pine nuts, walnuts, and oil and process until puréed. Add the cheese and process briefly, until thoroughly combined. Taste and season with additional salt, if needed, and pepper. Turn into a bowl and set aside; the pesto can be made ahead, covered, and refrigerated for a couple of days or frozen indefinitely.

In a large pot of salted boiling water, cook the fusilli until just *al dente*. Drain and rinse under cold water to stop the cooking. Transfer the pasta to a bowl of cold water and let cool to room temperature.

Prepare the salad: In a large bowl, combine the zucchini and onions. Drain the pasta very well and toss it with the vegetables. Pour on the pesto and toss until the pasta is well coated. Taste and adjust the seasonings if necessary. Serve at room temperature or chilled.

Serves 10 to 12

TOMATO, RED ONION, AND BASIL SALAD WITH MIB'S VINAIGRETTE

Nothing beats a simple salad with a terrific-tasting dressing. Mib's Vinaigrette has become a standard in my home. The recipe was given to me by my London-based friend, Isabel Bird.

SALAD

    5 to 6 large ripe tomatoes, sliced or cut
        into wedges
    1 to 2 large red onions, thinly sliced and
        separated into rings
    1 cup fresh basil leaves

MIB'S VINAIGRETTE

    ¼ cup white wine vinegar
    1 tablespoon plus 1 teaspoon Dijon
        mustard
    3 garlic cloves, minced
    2 teaspoons chopped fresh thyme, or 1
        teaspoon dried thyme
    2 teaspoons salt
    ¾ cup peanut oil
    ¾ cup olive oil

Arrange the tomatoes, onions, and basil on a platter or in a bowl.

Using a food processor or blender, or a jar with a tight-fitting lid, combine the vinegar, mustard, garlic, thyme, and salt and mix well. Add the oils in a slow stream and blend until thoroughly mixed.

Pour the vinaigrette over the salad and serve.

Serves 10 to 12

KATHLEEN'S DEVIL'S FOOD CAKE

Kathleen King runs Kathleen's Cookies on Long Island. It's one of my family's favorite stops.

CAKE

    ½ pound (2 sticks) unsalted butter, at
        room temperature
    3½ cups tightly packed light brown sugar
    3 large eggs
    3 1-ounce squares unsweetened
        chocolate, melted and cooled
    2 cups sifted cake flour
    2 teaspoons baking soda
    ½ teaspoon salt
    ½ cup buttermilk
    1 cup boiling water
    2 teaspoons vanilla extract

CHOCOLATE BUTTER-CREAM FROSTING

    ½ pound (2 sticks) unsalted butter,
        softened
    7 cups (2 pounds) confectioners' sugar
    6 1-ounce squares unsweetened
        chocolate, melted and cooled
    ½ cup buttermilk
    ¼ cup Kahlua or other coffee-flavored
        liqueur
    1 tablespoon vanilla extract

Preheat the oven to 375°F. Butter and flour two 9-inch round cake pans.

Make the cake: In a large bowl, cream together the butter and brown sugar. One at a time, add the eggs, beating well after each addition. Stir in the chocolate.

On a sheet of wax paper, sift together the cake flour, baking soda, and salt. One-third at a time, add the dry ingredients to the cake batter, alternating with the buttermilk. Pour in the boiling water and vanilla and beat until well combined and smooth.

Divide the batter between the prepared pans and bake for 25 to 35 minutes, or until a toothpick inserted in the center comes out clean. Remove to wire racks and let the cake layers cool completely. Remove from the pans.

Make the frosting: In a large bowl, cream together the butter and confectioners' sugar. Add the chocolate and beat until well mixed. Slowly add the buttermilk, Kahlua, and vanilla and beat until thick and smooth.

Place one cake layer on a cake platter. Spread about one-quarter of the frosting on top of the bottom layer and set the top layer in place. Frost the top and sides of the cake.

Fit a pastry bag with a decorative tip and fill it with the remaining frosting. Pipe a border around the base of the cake and decorate the top to suit the occasion.

Serves 8 to 12

Note: If not decorating the cake, halve the frosting ingredients.

CHRIS MEAD

MARY'S BIRTHDAY
WEEKEND

※ ※ ※ ※

Come Sunday morning, especially after a big bash the night before, everybody likes to move around at his own pace, and I have arrived at the perfect routine for providing for guests with a minimum of fuss. It's called serve-yourself brunch.

The menu makes use of farm-fresh eggs, fruits of the season, and leftovers. The key is organizing everything ahead of time. For me, that means baking enough loaves of potato bread on Friday to carry us through the weekend. Then, before going to bed Saturday night, I get everything assembled—coffee, fruit, and all the fixings for a frittata, which I will fill with red pepper and asparagus (or potatoes and cheese —whatever is left over from supper).

In the morning, I put out the bread and my old-fashioned milk bottle carrier (one of many that I collect and am constantly finding new uses for) filled with jams, honeys, and fancy sugars.

Early risers usually plug in the coffee and walk down the street to fetch a Sunday paper. Sometimes they also return with a bouquet of fresh flowers and that goes on the table, too. By the time the rest of the house is up, everyone is ready to sit down to enjoy a brunch that is as easy as boiling eggs and sautéing homegrown vegetables for the frittata.

※ ※ ※ ※

The shingle-style house is traditional in rural Long Island.

MENU

SERVE-YOURSELF SUNDAY BRUNCH

Fresh-Squeezed Orange Juice

Soft-Cooked Eggs

Asparagus, Onion, and Red Pepper Frittata

Long Island New Potato Bread

Honey-Sweetened Jams

Melon Wedges

Peaches or Nectarines

Coffee

❀❀❀❀❀

There's room for everybody in this farmhouse kitchen (above), where pillows match the pink of Mary's favorite antique Staffordshire china. The soft-boiled eggs in cups have sprigs of fresh tarragon on the side. A barrel of geraniums (right) supplies summer-long color on the brick patio.

Country lounges made of twig (above) have matching homespun cushions and pillows. Carved early American flag makes a patriotic garden gate (right).

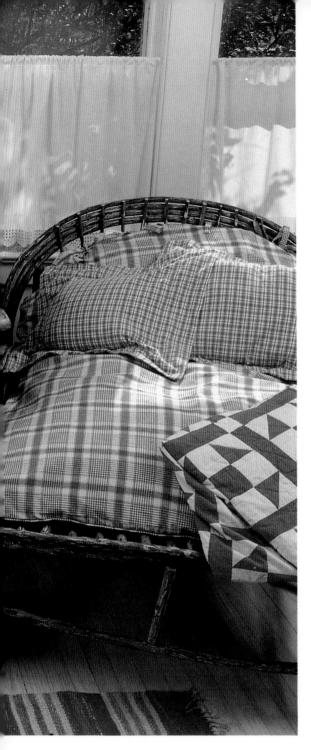

ASPARAGUS, ONION, AND RED PEPPER FRITTATA

This frittata could be served for breakfast, lunch, or dinner, depending on the accompaniments. Substitute whatever fresh vegetables are in season.

2 tablespoons olive oil

1 small onion, chopped

6 large eggs

1 teaspoon Tabasco sauce
  Salt and freshly ground black pepper

6 to 8 asparagus spears, stems peeled if
  large, and blanched or steamed briefly

6 bacon slices, cut into 1-inch pieces and
  fried

1 sweet red pepper, cored, seeded, and
  cut into julienne

Preheat the oven to 375°F.

In a heavy medium skillet, warm the olive oil over moderate heat. Add the onion and sauté until soft and golden, 3 to 5 minutes.

In a bowl, beat together the eggs and Tabasco sauce. Season with salt and pepper to taste.

Pour the eggs into a heart-shaped or round ovenproof baking pan and place in the oven for 3 minutes. Remove from the oven and arrange the asparagus, bacon, and red pepper strips attractively over the eggs.

Return the pan to the oven and bake for 8 to 10 minutes, or until the bottom is browned and the eggs are set.

Turn the oven to broil and slide under the broiler for 2 to 3 minutes until nicely browned on top. Cut into wedges and serve.

Serves 4 to 6

LONG ISLAND NEW POTATO BREAD

2 packages active dry yeast

½ cup lukewarm milk (105° to 115°F.)

8 cups bread flour

2 tablespoons salt

1½ cups mashed, cooked new potatoes

4 tablespoons (½ stick) unsalted butter,
  softened

2 cups lukewarm water (105° to 115°F.)
  Vegetable oil for the bowl

In a small bowl, dissolve the yeast in the warm milk and set aside to proof.

In a large bowl, sift together the flour and salt. Rub in the mashed potatoes and butter with the back of a wooden spoon until the mixture resembles coarse bread crumbs.

Form a well in the center of the flour mixture and pour in the warm water and the yeast. Mix until a stiff dough forms. Knead for 10 minutes on a lightly floured board, until pliable.

Coat a large clean bowl with oil. Place the dough in the bowl and turn to coat it with the oil. Cover the bowl with a towel and set in a warm, draft-free place to rise until the dough doubles in size, 1½ to 2 hours. Punch down the dough, cover with a damp towel, and allow to rise again by half, about 1 hour.

Preheat the oven to 400°F. Shape the dough into a disc and place on a lightly floured baking sheet. Bake for 1 hour, or until the bread is golden brown and sounds hollow when tapped on the bottom.

Makes 1 free-form loaf

MENU

SAMANTHA AND JONATHAN'S "SPECIAL TREAT"

Raspberry Cheesecake Pie

Secret Recipe Lemonade

❦❦❦❦❦❦❦

*An impromptu late-afternoon
snack for the Emmerling family
has been turned into a
special treat with the help of
flowers, tablecloth, and a pretty
paper doily.*

MARY'S BIRTHDAY WEEKEND

Early Sunday afternoon, life begins to settle back to normal—that means the children and often a friend or two are manning their stand, rounding up customers for their Secret Recipe Lemonade.

The village of Bridgehampton is small-town America in a nutshell, with a Main Street where every face is familiar and transactions for an ice-cream soda at the Candy Kitchen or the local paper at the drugstore are conducted on a friendly, first-name basis. For Samantha and Jonathan, a busy corner on Main Street provides the logical site for their lemonade stand every year. Here, they plunge into the world of commerce as much to chat with passersby as to earn money to replenish their stock of Archie and GI Joe comic books. But to be honest, the kids' enthusiasm for business usually lasts as long as it takes them to eat the bag of cookies they bring along with them to their prime retail location— usually about an hour.

I always have a special treat ready for the children when they come home with their friends to swim or play badminton. My life is impromptu during the summer, so I shop daily, relying on the fruit and vegetable farmstands for which Long Island is justly famous. Like everyone out here at this time of the year, I feast on the local corn, potatoes, tomatoes, and squashes. Then there are the berries, especially raspberries, a favorite of mine and the children's. I can never resist taking home a locally baked cheesecake pie topped with the biggest, sweetest raspberries of the season.

CHRIS MEAD

Samantha and Jonathan, with pal Edward Martin, offer patented lemonade to passersby.

CHRIS MEAD

RASPBERRY CHEESECAKE PIE

*If you prefer baking your own or don't have a
farmstand supply nearby, here's a recipe for
delectable cheesecake pie nourished with
raspberries.*

PASTRY

- 1⅓ cups all-purpose flour
- ½ teaspoon salt
- ½ cup shortening
- 3 to 4 tablespoons ice water

FILLING

- 1 8-ounce package cream cheese, softened
- 6 tablespoons (¾ stick) unsalted butter, softened
- ⅔ cup sugar
- 2 eggs, at room temperature
- 1 tablespoon framboise or framboise liqueur
- Pinch of salt

FRUIT AND GLAZE

- 3 pints fresh raspberries
- 1 cup apricot preserves
- 1 tablespoon framboise or framboise liqueur

Make the pastry: In a bowl, combine
the flour and salt. Using a pastry
blender or two knives, cut in the shortening until the mixture resembles
coarse meal. One tablespoon at a time,
add the ice water and mix just until the
pastry holds together.

Form the pastry into a flat disc and
cover with plastic wrap. Refrigerate for
at least 30 minutes.

Preheat the oven to 375°F.

On a floured surface, roll out the
pastry into a thin round. Fit the pastry
into an 8- or 9-inch pie pan. Trim and
crimp the edges. Line the pastry with a
sheet of aluminum foil and add aluminum baking weights, dried beans, or
rice to weight it down.

Bake in the center of the oven for 8
to 10 minutes, or until the edges are
lightly browned. Remove the weights
and foil and bake for 2 to 3 minutes
more, or until the pastry is no longer
moist and is lightly browned.

Set the pie shell on a wire rack and
allow to cool to room temperature.

Make the filling: Preheat the oven to
375°F. In a food processor fitted with
a metal blade or with an electric mixer,
combine the cream cheese, butter, and
sugar until well blended. One at a time,
add the eggs and beat until fluffy. Beat
in the framboise and salt.

Pour the filling into the cooled pie
shell and bake in the center of the oven
for 25 to 30 minutes, or until lightly
browned on top. Remove to a wire rack
to cool completely to room temperature. Cover and refrigerate if not adding the berries until later.

Assemble the pie: Pick over the berries, reserving any imperfect ones for
the bottom layer or for another use.
Generously mound the berries over the
cooled cheesecake.

Make the glaze: In a small saucepan, melt the apricot preserves over low heat. Strain the preserves through a fine sieve to remove the solids. Stir the framboise into the strained apricot glaze. Brush the glaze over the berries and piecrust, coating them completely. Serve at once, or cover and chill until serving time.

Serves 6 to 8

SECRET RECIPE LEMONADE

Good lemonade requires lots of ice and then sugar to taste. A big bowl of superfine sugar on the table will give everyone a chance to make the lemonade as tart or sweet as he or she likes.

12 large lemons
 1 orange
   Superfine sugar
   Ice

Wash the lemons and orange. Halve the fruit and remove the seeds. Squeeze the juice from the fruit and add the juice and squeezed fruit to a large pitcher. Chill until serving time.

Add a generous amount of ice cubes to the pitcher and stir to dilute the lemonade. Or add 5 to 6 cups cold water or seltzer and pour into ice-filled glasses. Serve with sugar on the side so each person can sweeten his or her own.

Serves 10 to 12

Cheesecake pie with glazed raspberry topping is ready for serving on blue willowware dishes, along with the children's own lemonade to quench thirsts.

BOAT PICNIC WITH MARY AND FRIENDS

Sag Harbor, Long Island

MENU

Smoked Chicken Salad

Fusilli and Feta with Fresh Sorrel

Cucumber Salad with Fresh Dill

Sesame-Broccoli Salad

Bucheron Cheese with Herbs

French Bread

Peach Tart

Blueberry Tart

Champagne

I'm basically a landlubber, but even I can't resist the call of the sea when it comes from Tom Reeves, "captain" of a handsome old wood sailboat named *Clover*, berthed in neighboring Sag Harbor, Long Island. When Tom, a good friend of my brother Terry's, invites me and my friends to join him for a day of sailing, I always insist on bringing the food. All I need to fill my baskets with an array of fresh salads, pastries, and homemade breads is a stop at my favorite local gourmet carryout, Loaves & Fishes. (All the recipes here are from their cookbook.) Then, with a menu that materializes out of take-home containers, I transfer the food onto china plates, spread the linens, and bring out the silver ice bucket. That's all it takes to turn the deck of the *Clover* into an elegant picnic site.

Becalmed Long Island Sound offers a surface as smooth as glass for a casual banquet at sea (left), supplied by Mary Emmerling and Loaves & Fishes (right).

SMOKED CHICKEN SALAD

Make this salad up to eight hours before you need it so that all the flavors have time to blend.

- 3 boned smoked chicken breasts (about 2½ pounds)
- 1 medium onion, peeled and minced
- 1 red pepper, sliced into ½-inch pieces
- ¾ cup fresh shelled peas
- ½ cup finely chopped parsley

DRESSING

- ⅔ cup mayonnaise
- 2 teaspoons white wine vinegar
- 1 teaspoon salt
- 1 teaspoon ground black pepper

Remove the skin and fat from the smoked chicken breasts. Cut the chicken into bite-size chunks and place in a salad bowl. Add the onion, red pepper, peas, and parsley.

To make the dressing, mix the ingredients in a separate bowl, then pour over the chicken. Blend well with your hands.

Serves 6

FUSILLI AND FETA WITH FRESH SORREL

- ¾ pound fusilli noodles
- ¾ pound feta cheese, cut into ½-inch cubes
- ¼ cup peeled and minced red onion
- ½ cup diced sun-dried tomatoes, drained
- 1 cup Niçoise black olives, pitted
- 3 cups fresh sorrel leaves

DRESSING

- 1 clove garlic, peeled and minced
- ½ teaspoon salt
- ¾ teaspoon pepper
- 3 tablespoons red wine vinegar
- ½ cup olive oil

Boil the fusilli until just done, about 10 minutes. Drain and transfer to a mixing bowl. Add the feta cheese, onion, tomatoes, olives, and sorrel.

To make the dressing, combine all the ingredients in a container with a lid and shake well. Pour the dressing over the salad and mix lightly with your hands. Serve at room temperature.

Serves 6 to 8

CUCUMBER SALAD WITH FRESH DILL

- 2 European cucumbers
- 1 teaspoon salt
- 2 cloves garlic, peeled and minced
- ½ cup peeled and finely chopped red onion
- ¼ cup chopped dill
- 1 teaspoon sugar
- 1 teaspoon ground white pepper
- 2 tablespoons white wine vinegar
- 1½ cups sour cream

Slice the cucumbers very thin. Sprinkle with salt and place them in a colander for 15 minutes. Then press out as much liquid as you can with the back of a large spoon. Transfer the cucumber slices to a salad bowl. Add the rest of the ingredients and mix gently but thoroughly with your hands. The salad will keep for up to 24 hours in the refrigerator.

Serves 6 to 8

SESAME-BROCCOLI SALAD

- 2 heads of broccoli
- ¼ cup sesame oil
- 2 teaspoons hot red pepper flakes

DRESSING

- 2 cloves garlic, peeled and minced
- 1 teaspoon salt
- 2 tablespoons red wine vinegar
- ⅓ cup olive oil

Cut off the broccoli tops into 2½-inch-long florets and place them in a mixing bowl. Peel the stems, discarding the lower woody part, and cut them into bite-size pieces. Place with the florets.

Heat the sesame oil over a medium flame to the point just before it starts to smoke. Remove from the heat, add the hot red pepper flakes, and allow them to steep for 10 minutes. Then pour the oil over the broccoli.

To make the dressing, combine the ingredients in a container with a tight-fitting lid. Shake vigorously and pour over the salad. Toss well, using your hands. Marinate for 2 hours in the refrigerator.

Serves 6

BUCHERON CHEESE WITH HERBS

- 2 cups good, fruity olive oil
- 3 cloves garlic, peeled and halved
- ¼ cup minced fresh parsley
- ¼ cup minced fresh chives
- 3 tablespoons minced fresh basil
- 1 teaspoon dried thyme
- 1 teaspoon ground black pepper
- 1¼ pounds Bucheron goat cheese, left whole or cut into ½-inch slices

Heat the olive oil in a saucepan until it starts to smoke. Remove it from the heat and let it stand for 10 minutes. Stir in the garlic, parsley, chives, basil, thyme, and pepper. Let it cool to room temperature.

Place the Bucheron in a serving bowl and pour the oil and herb mixture over it. Cover and refrigerate for at least 3 days. (The cheese will keep for a week or more in the refrigerator.) Bring to room temperature before serving.

Serves 6 to 8

Plates and bowls with anchor monogram await a serving of summer salads and fruit tarts. Crusty French bread accompanies a strong herb-flavored Bucheron.

COOL SUMMER DAYS IN MAINE

Kennebunkport, Maine

Steamed while you wait at a lobster shack (above), the shellfish dinner synonymous with the state of Maine will be served with fresh corn purchased at a farm stand by the fields (right).

HARBORSIDE LOBSTER DINNER

I reserve the pleasure of eating my first lobster of the summer for my annual sojourn in Maine. The snug harbor town of Kennebunkport, with its charming eighteenth- and nineteenth-century sea captains' mansions, is my favorite destination.

While it's enjoyable to dine on lobster at one of the picturesque clapboard roadside shacks that specialize in this fare or to prepare it native style in a seaweed-packed pit right on the beach, you can cook the shellfish at home and still enjoy it to the hilt.

This primitive crustacean is the ultimate in finger food for me. The twisting, cracking, and digging required to extract the sweet meat from the shells and claws is part of the sport of lobster eating and is best reserved for an outdoor location.

Lobster, when steamed or boiled to a crimson red in four inches of water (seawater direct from the Atlantic Ocean if it's handy, advise the natives), served with native corn, coleslaw, and plenty of melted butter, and accompanied by paper napkins, is the original New England shore dinner.

Bait, buoys, and pots for catching Maine lobster are stored at a shack by the scenic coastline (left). The classic Maine lobster meal (below) is served outside without fuss or pretension, preferably using tableware that can be discarded with the shells.

BOILED LOBSTER

You can make lobster at home the way the pros do in little lobster shacks along the New England coast.

1 1¼- to 1½-pound live lobster
Melted unsalted butter

In a pot, bring a large quantity of water to a boil over high heat. If desired, you may add seaweed to the pot. Plunge the lobster, head first, into the boiling water and cover. Cook for 13 minutes. Remove and drain at once.

Serve hot, with hot melted butter.

Serves 1

Make-at-home additions to the bounty of the field and sea: red and white cabbage are combined in a crunchy coleslaw (above) and a flaky puff pastry surrounds blueberries in this easy-to-make cobbler (right).

CREAMY COLESLAW

Slightly sweet and soothing flavors mingle to make this all-American coleslaw.

1 head green cabbage, coarsely shredded
2 carrots, peeled and shredded
1 cup sour cream
½ cup mayonnaise
2 tablespoons white wine vinegar
2 tablespoons milk
1½ tablespoons sugar
2 teaspoons celery seeds
2 teaspoons freshly ground black pepper
1 teaspoon salt
½ to 1 teaspoon Tabasco sauce

In a large bowl, toss the cabbage with the carrots to mix the colors.

In another bowl, whisk together the sour cream, mayonnaise, vinegar, milk, sugar, celery seeds, pepper, salt, and Tabasco sauce until smooth.

Pour the dressing over the slaw and toss to coat well. Cover and refrigerate until serving time. Serve cold.

Serves 4 to 6

BLUEBERRY COBBLER

2 cups blueberries
About ¼ cup sugar
1 tablespoon cornstarch
1 pound frozen puff pastry, thawed according to package directions

Preheat the oven to 425°F.

In a nonreactive saucepan, combine the blueberries and the sugar over moderate heat. Cook, stirring, until the berries burst and the sugar is melted. The juice will be somewhat thick, the fruit relatively soft.

In a small bowl, stir together the cornstarch and 1 tablespoon cold water until smooth. Add to the fruit and cook for about 3 minutes until the juices are thick and shiny. Set aside.

On a lightly floured surface, unwrap the pastry and cut it into four equal squares. Lightly roll out each square to make it slightly larger. Fit each square in a custard cup, with the center of the square in the bottom and the edges falling over the sides of the cup. Divide the fruit mixture among the cups and place the cups several inches apart on a baking sheet.

Bake for 15 minutes. Reduce the oven temperature to 350°F. and bake for about 15 minutes more, until the pastry is puffed and browned.

Serve hot or at room temperature.

Serves 4

The panorama of the Maine coast
would not be complete without
boats, both in the water (above)
and on land (right).

SEPTEMBER IN TEXAS AND NEW MEXICO

WILD GAME COOKOUT AT BEVERLY AND DAVID CUMMINGS'

Junction, Texas

MENU

Mesquite-Grilled Blackbuck Antelope, Axis Deer, and Cabrito

Barbecue Sauce for Mopping

Barbecue Sauce for Eating

Savory Coleslaw

Pickled Vegetables

Mexican-Style Beans

Chile Salsa with Tomatoes

Corn Pudding

Jalapeño Corn-Bread Muffins

Mexican Chocolate Sheet Cake

Lone Star Draught Beer

Artesian Spring Water

The cookers were smoking, flavoring the air with pungent mesquite. The Rounders, a local country-western group, strummed their guitars. Dozens of bales of hay, wrapped in burlap—the ranch foreman's idea of rustic furniture—dotted the sprawling lawn. The pickups and Cadillacs wound their way toward this welcoming scene at a ranch house in rural Junction, Texas. Overhead, the stars were beginning to come out. The party, for 250 guests, was about to get under way.

This weekend gathering, hosted by Beverly and David Cummings, weekday residents of Houston, was as homey as a backyard barbecue, even though the backyard is three thousand acres of grassland and woods, a hundred miles west of San Antonio, known as the Dominion Ranch. Beverly's sure touch in handling large groups of people, combined with the Texas-size setting of the ranch and a menu that is decidedly "on the wild side," elevate this annual September gathering into a not-to-be-missed event on the social calendars of the Cummingses' friends from all over the state.

Dedicated conservationists, the cou-

Wagon wheel and skull are reminders of the era of the region's early settlers.

Gathered around a sprawling stone ranch house in the Hill Country of Texas, friends from all over the state kick off an evening of mesquite-flavored socializing with a cookout under the stars.

ple acquired their property six years ago, not to use as a commercial working ranch, but to create a refuge for wildlife. In addition to native species like whitetail deer and wild turkeys, the Cummingses have stocked their ranch with such exotic animals as Russian boar, blackbuck antelope, Oriental Sika deer, Axis deer, and Aoudad, a wild sheep from North Africa. They built lakes and planted special grasses to provide the best possible habitat for the animals. Game hunting is prohibited but the herds are culled from time to time to keep their numbers at a healthy level. As a result, the Cummingses are able to offer their guests such far-out fare as mesquite-grilled blackbuck, Sika deer sausages, and spit-roasted wild boar. The year I attended, more than three hundred pounds of meat was barbecued!

Large-scale entertaining can be the undoing of a party-giver and this cook-out could not have succeeded without the careful planning that began a full year in advance. Beverly's leather-bound notebook, bulging with notes and reminders, is the key. "I keep my permanent guest list in here, which I update and add to regularly," she says. "In another section of the notebook, I keep an idea file for the ranch party, lists of past menus, and notes on items that might be suitable for party favors or props." Beverly mails formal invitations two months before the event, but sends out "preinvitation announcements" even earlier so friends will remember to keep the September date clear. In Texas' sesquicentennial year, she reproduced an artist friend's rendering of the siege of the Alamo on postcards and sent them out with the message: "Remember the Alamo and don't forget the Dominion Ranch Party a hundred and fifty years later!"

An inveterate collector, Beverly has assembled a wide variety of objects, including wildlife paintings, fish trophies, whimsical mottoware from England,

pink-and-white masonware, and books and emblems of old Texas. In her Houston home, she maintains a "prop closet," a room with stored collections of bandannas, baskets, and other items Beverly draws upon to decorate the ranch parties. One year, for example, a group of old cheese graters was transformed into *luminarias* that provided romantic lighting for the outdoor tables.

Another year, tissue-paper floral bouquets were fashioned into centerpieces for the tables. "But we set them out too soon," Beverly relates. It turns out some of God's creatures were attracted by these colorful props: "The deer came in and ate them!"

───────

The custom-built cooker (left) uses slow-burning mesquite for fuel; a large pan of water placed over the fire helps generate moist smoke, which bastes meat as it cooks. A tray with silver longhorn handles (above) is heaped with exotic fare: Sika deer sausages and barbecued blackbuck venison.

MESQUITE-GRILLED BLACKBUCK ANTELOPE, AXIS DEER, AND CABRITO

If you have the good fortune to have access to wild game, you'll probably develop a taste for its flavorful sweet meat. What's most important is knowing how to cook it. Beverly and David Cummings know how.

A dressed blackbuck antelope yields the backstrap (boneless tenderloin) and an 8- to 10-pound ham. The ham of an Axis deer has good color that is well marbled, similar to aged beef. When cooked, it retains lots of moisture and flavor.

To grill blackbuck antelope and Axis deer, soak the meat in a marinade of dry red wine, mashed garlic cloves, chopped onions, and celery tops, seasoned with bay leaves, thyme, sage, and ground cloves and nutmeg. In a large barbecue grill or pit, place the meat at the opposite end from the fire and set a pan of water directly over the fire. Cover and avoid opening during the cooking. Cook for 30 minutes per pound; the water will create moist smoke which will "baste" the meat as it cooks.

Cabrito is Spanish kid that is less than 1 year old and not over 15 pounds. Cook it slowly, turning and basting frequently with the mopping sauce, over a low mesquite fire for 8 to 10 hours, until it is tender and cooked through.

───────

BARBECUE SAUCE FOR MOPPING

According to Beverly Cummings, there are two types of barbecue sauce: one for mopping the meat while it cooks and another one for eating. The rule to follow is: "Never mop with an eating sauce and never eat with a mopping sauce."

This sauce is especially good for game and red meat.

½ pound (2 sticks) unsalted butter

4 cups cider vinegar

2 cups vegetable oil

2 cups fresh lemon juice

2 cups Worcestershire sauce

1 cup prepared mustard

1 medium onion, minced

2 to 3 garlic cloves, minced

2 tablespoons cayenne pepper

2 tablespoons salt

1 tablespoon freshly ground black
    pepper

In a large nonaluminum saucepan, combine all of the ingredients over low heat. Simmer, stirring from time to time, for 1 hour.

Baste the meat with the mopping sauce as it cooks.

Makes about 3 quarts

BARBECUE SAUCE FOR EATING

Use this sauce as a condiment. It's good on hamburgers, steaks, or chicken.

8 tablespoons (1 stick) unsalted butter

1 medium onion, minced

1 garlic clove, minced

⅔ cup firmly packed brown sugar

¼ cup cider vinegar

¼ cup fresh lemon juice

2 tablespoons prepared mustard

1 5-ounce bottle A-1 Sauce

1 8-ounce can tomato sauce

1 12-ounce can V-8 juice

1 12-ounce bottle chili sauce

1 14-ounce bottle ketchup

In a large nonaluminum saucepan, melt the butter over moderate heat. Add the onion and garlic and sauté until soft, 3 to 5 minutes.

Add all of the remaining ingredients and turn the heat to low. Cook, stirring from time to time, for at least 3 hours, or until the flavors are well mingled and developed.

Let cool to room temperature, cover, and refrigerate if not using immediately.

Makes about 2 quarts

Two-cabbage coleslaw and vegetables pickled in vinegar (right) are colorful dishes native to the region. Shed antlers left to bleach on the verandah won't scare a family pet from its napping spot (below).

SAVORY COLESLAW

½ large head red cabbage, finely shredded
½ large head white cabbage, finely
    shredded
2 carrots, shredded
½ cup white wine vinegar
¼ cup sugar
1 tablespoon Dijon mustard
2 teaspoons celery seeds
1 teaspoon salt
¾ cup light vegetable oil

In a large bowl, combine the cabbages and the carrots. Toss to mix the colors.

In a jar with a tight-fitting lid, combine the vinegar, sugar, mustard, celery seeds, and salt. Cover and shake to dissolve the sugar. Add the oil and cover again. Shake very well. Pour the dressing over the cabbage and carrots and toss. Set aside to "wilt" a bit before serving or refrigerate.

Serves 8

MEXICAN-STYLE BEANS

These beans improve with age. Feel free to make them two to three days before you plan to serve them. Let the beans come to room temperature, cover, and refrigerate. Reheat over moderate heat until hot. Never add salt until shortly before serving time or the beans will toughen.

2 pounds dried pinto beans
1 ham bone, or 1 2-inch piece of salt
    pork
1 large onion, chopped
2 large garlic cloves, minced
1 14-ounce can Rotel tomatoes, if
    available, or 1 14-ounce can Italian
    plum tomatoes and 2 tablespoons
    chopped green chiles
¼ cup chopped fresh cilantro (coriander)
2 tablespoons chili powder
2 teaspoons ground cumin
1 teaspoon sugar
    Salt

Pick over the pinto beans, removing any small pebbles or rocks; then wash the beans. In a large nonreactive pot, soak the beans in ample water to cover for 8 hours or overnight.

Place the pot of beans over moderately high heat and add the ham bone, onion, garlic, and tomatoes. Stir in the cilantro, chili powder, cumin, and sugar and bring to a simmer.

Turn the heat to low, cover, and cook for about 4 hours, or until the beans are tender.

About 15 minutes before serving, season with salt to taste. Serve hot.

Serves 10 to 12

Burlap-wrapped bales of fresh hay provide cowpoke-style seating (top) at the annual cookout hosted by Beverly and David Cummings. "Dress blue" in Texas means denim jeans and skirts for most guests (above left). Country-western music sets the friendly tone (above right). Mark White, former governor of Texas (below), is just "one of the cowboys" at a country barbecue.

CHILE SALSA WITH TOMATOES

This sauce is good enough to have in your refrigerator at all times. Beverly Cummings likes to use it on just about everything—from steaks to scrambled eggs—or just as a side dish.

> 2 tablespoons vegetable oil
> 1 medium onion, chopped
> 2 garlic cloves, minced
> 1 35-ounce can Italian plum tomatoes, or 5 large ripe tomatoes, peeled and coarsely chopped
> ⅓ to ½ cup chopped fresh green chiles, or 2 4-ounce cans chopped green chiles, drained
> 1 to 2 fresh jalapeño peppers, chopped (optional)
> 1 teaspoon salt
> 1 teaspoon dried oregano
> ½ teaspoon ground cumin

In a large skillet, warm the oil over moderate heat. Add the onion and garlic and sauté until soft, about 5 minutes.

Add all of the remaining ingredients and simmer, stirring from time to time, for 15 minutes.

Serve hot, at room temperature, or cold.

Makes about 4 cups

CORN PUDDING

Carol Curry is the proprietor of the Old Republic Inn in Kerrville, Texas, a small restaurant that serves lunch daily and caters special functions in the Junction area. This is her recipe for smooth, sweet, delicious corn pudding.

> 1 17-ounce can creamed-style corn
> 1 17-ounce can whole-kernel corn, drained
> 2 large eggs, beaten
> ½ cup milk
> ¼ cup sugar
> 1 tablespoon all-purpose flour
> ¼ teaspoon salt
> 1 tablespoon unsalted butter, cut into bits

Preheat the oven to 350°F. Generously butter a 1-quart round casserole or baking dish.

In a large bowl, combine the creamed corn, whole corn, eggs, and milk. Add the sugar, flour, and salt and stir to mix thoroughly. Pour the pudding into the prepared casserole and dot with the butter. Bake in the center of the oven for 1 hour.

Pour off any excess liquid and set the casserole aside to allow the pudding to set. Serve hot, at room temperature, or cold.

Serves 6 to 8

Heart-shaped dinner bell is rung with a tin star (below). Graceful stag on weather vane is emblematic of the game herds roaming the ranch (bottom).

Corn-bread muffins, flavored with the locals' beloved jalapeño peppers, are coddled in bandanna-lined baskets.

JALAPEÑO CORN-BREAD MUFFINS

If you think jalapeños are a bit too hot, substitute green chiles in their place.

> 1 cup yellow cornmeal
> ½ teaspoon salt
> 1 tablespoon baking powder
> ⅓ cup melted bacon fat or shortening
> 2 large eggs, beaten
> 1 cup cream-style canned corn
> 1 cup sour cream, or
>   ⅔ cup buttermilk
> 1 medium onion, chopped
> 1 cup shredded sharp Cheddar cheese
> 4 to 6 fresh or canned jalapeño peppers,
>   or 1 4-ounce can chopped green
>   chiles, drained

Preheat the oven to 350°F. Lightly oil a 12-cup muffin tin.

In a large bowl, combine the cornmeal, salt and baking powder. Stir in the bacon fat. Add the eggs, creamed corn, and sour cream and blend well. Stir in the onion.

Fill each muffin cup with 2 to 3 tablespoons of butter. Sprinkle on the cheese and jalapeños and top each with a smooth layer of the remaining batter.

Bake for 35 to 40 minutes, or until a toothpick inserted in the center of a muffin comes out clean.

Allow the muffins to cool and remove from the cups.

Makes 12 muffins

Cobbler's shoe-drying rack stores antlers, Mexican pottery, and a steepled birdhouse.

MEXICAN CHOCOLATE SHEET CAKE

The chocolate, coffee, and cinnamon flavors really come through in this cake. It is a strikingly simple dessert, but the tastes make it seem difficult and complex.

CAKE

- 8 tablespoons (1 stick) unsalted butter
- ¼ cup unsweetened cocoa powder
- 2 cups all-purpose flour
- 2 cups granulated sugar
- ½ cup buttermilk
- 2 large eggs
- 1 teaspoon baking soda
- 1 teaspoon vanilla extract
- 1 teaspoon ground cinnamon
- 1 teaspoon powdered instant espresso or regular coffee
- ½ teaspoon salt
- ¾ cup chopped walnuts or pecans (optional)

ICING

- 3½ cups (1 16-ounce box) confectioners' sugar
- 8 tablespoons (1 stick) unsalted butter, melted
- ¼ cup unsweetened cocoa powder
- ¼ cup plus 2 tablespoons milk
- 1 teaspoon vanilla extract
- 1 teaspoon powdered instant espresso or regular coffee
- 1 teaspoon ground cinnamon

Preheat the oven to 400°F. Butter and flour a 15 x 10 x 2-inch baking dish or pan.

Make the cake: In a small saucepan, combine the butter, cocoa, and 1 cup of water over moderate heat. Bring to a boil and remove from the heat.

In a large bowl, sift together the flour and granulated sugar. Add the melted cocoa mixture and beat with an electric mixer at medium speed until well blended.

Continue beating and add the buttermilk, eggs, baking soda, vanilla, cinnamon, instant coffee, and salt. The batter will be light. Fold in the nuts.

Pour the batter into the prepared pan and bake for 20 minutes. The cake will be very moist. Remove to a wire rack to cool.

Make the icing: In a large bowl, combine the confectioners' sugar, melted butter, cocoa, and milk. Mix well and stir in the vanilla, instant coffee, and cinnamon.

When the cake has cooled for 15 to 20 minutes, spread the icing over the cake while it is still warm. Serve the cake, cut into squares, warm or at room temperature.

Serves 12 to 16

Chocolate sheet cake, cut into chunky squares (above), has been prepared Mexican style, with ground cinnamon and powdered coffee added to the flour. Visitors to the 3,000-acre Dominion Ranch of Beverly and David Cummings are greeted by a Texas-size vista (below).

Fredericksburg, Texas

POTLUCK SOCIAL AT CHERI AND BOBBY CARTER'S

MENU

Creek Soup

Copper Pennies

Mesquite-Grilled Beef
Tenderloin

Opa's Sausages

Golden Eggplant Casserole

Fruit Salad with Honey-
Lime Dressing

Mixed Fruit Tart

Cinnamon-Crumb-Topped
Apple Pie

A potluck supper at Cheri and Bob Carter's 1889 limestone rock house (right) is a chance to enjoy some down-home fiddle music while exchanging gossip and family recipes. Cheri prepares the Texas-style wine cooler (above).

The potluck supper is one of our most pleasant and practical traditions for sharing homemade foods with friends and neighbors. In the small family-oriented community of Fredericksburg, Texas, Cheri and Bobby Carter have raised potluck to an art and dressed it in Country finery.

"It's something we do a lot of around here," says Cheri. "Originally, the potluck supper was an inexpensive way for country folk to entertain. Few people had the means to invite twenty friends over for dinner, so families would pitch in with the cooking and bring it all to a common site down by the river or at the village church. Soon this gathering became a regular social event."

Then as now, potluck suppers required teamwork and coordination. "I'll set a date for the event, call up five or six couples, and ask each one to prepare a dish for six or eight servings." With this arrangement, no one becomes a slave to the kitchen, yet the buffet that results is richly varied "because everybody has a different approach to cooking," Cheri explains. "We usually end up with enough to serve twenty or thirty people. Plus, we

On a crocheted family heirloom
cloth, the desserts, casseroles, and
salads which neighbors have
brought over in their own favorite
containers show how fulfilling—
and filling—a potluck social
can be.

get to sample more than one kind of
salad and, better yet, more than one
dessert!"

As hosts, the Carters take responsi-
bility for the main meat course, almost
always a beef tenderloin grilled over
mesquite. "I believe in foolproof cooking," says Cheri. "I don't like to ex-
periment on guests. For me, tenderloin
is the easiest meat to prepare."

Cheri not only organizes the supper but also gives it style by drawing on her collections of quilts, antique linens, silver and glass goblets, and sets of old and new dishware. (Jabberwocky, her shop in Fredericksburg, is also a resource on these occasions.) "I don't like to spend hours in the kitchen, but I do fuss over the presentation," she says.

On the day of the supper, old tin washtubs are filled with wine, beer, and soda and brought outside. Tables are set up under the century-old hackberry trees on the lawn or on the porches of the main house and guest house. Both dwellings, hewn from indigenous limestone, date from the 1880s. A windmill and cistern, once used to supply the farm with water, provide a rustic backdrop for the gathering.

Quilts, pretty but not precious, serve as tablecloths. "When I'm using really valuable quilts," Cheri notes, "I never serve baked beans or red wine!"

Cheri insists on good linens at table. "There's nothing nicer than to sit down and put a freshly starched napkin in your lap," she says. "I also like the idea of setting off the simple food of the potluck supper with a Country elegant tablesetting. It makes everything seem that much more special."

CREEK SOUP

Trudy Harris has a pure flowing creek where she finds wild watercress as well as wild mint. On hot summer days, she and her guests have a great excuse to explore the creek—they're looking for greens for their soup. If you have no creek, the milder domestic watercress and mint will do nicely.

1 large bunch fresh watercress leaves

3 small sprigs fresh mint

1 medium potato, or 3 small new potatoes (about ½ pound total weight), cooked, peeled, and halved

2 scallions, trimmed and cut into chunks

2 cups chicken stock or broth

2 cups half-and-half

Juice of ½ large lemon

Dash of Tabasco sauce

Salt and freshly ground black pepper

Grated lemon rind for garnish

In a food processor fitted with a metal blade, combine the watercress leaves, mint leaves, potato, and scallions. Process until finely chopped.

Add the chicken stock, half-and-half, lemon juice, and Tabasco sauce and purée thoroughly. Season with salt and pepper to taste.

Cover and refrigerate until well chilled. Ladle into soup bowls or cups and garnish with finely grated lemon rind.

Serves 6 to 8

COPPER PENNIES

Jan Buehn's mother gave her this recipe, which will keep, refrigerated, for two weeks or more. The marinade closely resembles a Catalina or Russian dressing, and is delicious on a tossed salad.

5 cups sliced carrots, cut about ¼ inch thick (about 10 medium carrots)

1 large onion, thinly sliced

1 sweet green pepper, cored, seeded, and cut into thin strips

¾ cup cider vinegar

½ cup vegetable oil

2 8-ounce cans tomato sauce

1 teaspoon Worcestershire sauce

1 teaspoon powdered mustard

1 teaspoon celery seeds

1 teaspoon salt

½ teaspoon freshly ground black pepper

In a pot of boiling water, cook the carrots until barely tender. Drain well.

In a large nonreactive bowl, combine the carrots, onion, and green pepper.

In another bowl, combine the vinegar, oil, tomato sauce, Worcestershire sauce, mustard, celery seeds, salt, and pepper. Mix well.

Pour the dressing over the vegetables and toss to coat them well. Cover and refrigerate for at least 12 hours before serving cold.

Serves 12

Favorite family recipes are shared by the Harrises, left, and the Buehns, right. Trudy Harris mixes wild mint and watercress from the creek for an original chilled soup. Jan Buehn's carrot salad is tossed in a tangy tomato-based vinaigrette.

MESQUITE-GRILLED BEEF TENDERLOIN

Cheri Carter cooks beef tenderloin quickly over charcoal and mesquite and serves it at room temperature, cut into thick slices.

1 4- to 5-pound beef tenderloin, trimmed but leaving about ⅛ inch of fat on the top if possible (Ask your butcher to do this for you.)

1 thin sheet beef or pork fat (if tenderloin was thoroughly trimmed, optional)

1 garlic clove, halved

3 tablespoons olive oil

Freshly ground black pepper

½ pound (2 sticks) unsalted butter, softened

¼ to ½ cup minced fresh basil, dill, marjoram, or oregano, or 5 large garlic cloves, finely crushed

Sweet red peppers or tomatoes for garnish

Put a large quantity of mesquite chips in water to soak for about 1 hour. Meanwhile, put plenty of charcoal on one side of a grill and ignite it.

While the charcoal begins to burn, let the tenderloin come to room temperature. If the beef does not have a layer of fat attached, trim the sheet of beef or pork fat to fit and place on the top side of the tenderloin; tie at intervals with string. Rub the fat side with the cut halves of the garlic and coat the beef and fat with the oil. Sprinkle generously with pepper.

When the coals are very hot and ash covered, drain the mesquite chips and distribute them over the coals. Place the tenderloin, fat side down, on the other side of the grill and cover the grill. Adjust the air vents to maintain high heat without any open flame. Grill the meat for 15 minutes.

Turn the beef, adjusting the air vent to avoid flare-ups, if necessary. Grill for 15 minutes more for rare or about 20 minutes for medium-cooked beef.

While the meat grills, combine the butter with the minced herbs. Mix well to flavor the butter uniformly.

When the beef is cooked, remove it to a large platter. Spread the herb butter over the top and cover the meat with aluminum foil; the beef will continue to cook from its own heat. Set aside to come to room temperature. (The tenderloin can be grilled a day ahead of time, if desired. Refrigerate, covered, and let come to room temperature before slicing. Then melt the herb butter and pour it over the meat.)

To serve, cut the tenderloin into ½-inch-thick slices and arrange attractively on a serving platter. Spoon the pooled melted butter over the beef and garnish with red peppers or tomatoes.

Serves 8 to 12

A rock limestone cistern that originally supplied the house with water has been converted to an aboveground swimming hole.

In wooden-legged washtubs, beverages are iced down. Corkscrews and bottle openers are tied to western kerchiefs for easy handling (right). The porch of the tin-roofed guest cabin is a homey location for a table set for four (far right).

A kerosene lamp is a Country addition to an elegant table that mixes two patterns of family silver with hand-painted Minton china plates.

Gingham bows tied to table legs allow guests to maneuver without disturbing the quilt tops used as tablecloths.

GOLDEN EGGPLANT CASSEROLE

Nancy Wareing and her family have enjoyed this dish for twenty years or more. It resembles the filling for a quiche—easily put together and baked until set.

7½ to 8 cups peeled cubed eggplant
    (about 2 pounds)

54 Saltine crackers

1½ cups shredded sharp Cheddar cheese

¾ cup chopped celery

¼ cup plus 2 tablespoons chopped
    pimiento

3 tablespoons unsalted butter, melted

1½ teaspoons salt

½ teaspoon freshly ground black pepper

1½ cups half-and-half or evaporated milk

Lightly oil a 3-quart casserole or a 13 x 9 x 2-inch oblong baking dish.

Bring a large pot of salted water to a boil and cook the eggplant for 10 minutes. Drain well in a colander.

Preheat the oven to 350°F. Meanwhile, in a large bowl, combine the remaining ingredients. Add the eggplant and mix well.

Turn the mixture into the prepared casserole and bake for 45 minutes, or until golden brown on top and bubbling. Serve hot or at room temperature.

Serves 12

FRUIT SALAD WITH HONEY-LIME DRESSING

Betty Ethel takes advantage of whatever fruit is in season, though she's especially fond of using several types of melon in this salad. The dressing recipe can be cut down to serve four or tripled for fifty; leftover dressing will keep indefinitely if covered and refrigerated. It is delicious over a mixture of melon and blueberries.

SALAD

    Fresh strawberries, washed and hulled

    Watermelon, cut into bite-size chunks

    Honeydew melon, cut into bite-size
        chunks

    Cantaloupe, cut into bite-size chunks

    Kiwi fruit, peeled and thinly sliced
        into rounds

HONEY-LIME DRESSING

    ⅓ cup fresh lime juice

    ⅓ cup honey

    1 cup vegetable oil

    ½ cup dark rum (optional)

    ½ teaspoon paprika

    ½ teaspoon powdered mustard

    ½ teaspoon salt

    Grated rind of 1 lime

In a large serving bowl, combine all of the fruit. Cover and refrigerate.

In a small bowl, combine all of the dressing ingredients. Blend well, cover, and refrigerate.

Just before serving, pour the dressing over the fruit and toss to coat.

Makes about 2 cups dressing

The geese may be indifferent, but the golden eggplant casserole (above left) that Nancy Wareing makes is a family favorite. Betty Ethel enlivens her fresh fruit salad (above) with a honey-lime dressing spiked with rum.

MIXED FRUIT TART

This fruit tart, baked by Dr. Charles Schmidt, is based on a traditional German recipe.

DOUGH

- 2 cups all-purpose flour
- ¼ cup sugar
- 2 large egg yolks
- ½ pound (2 sticks) unsalted butter, melted

FILLING

- About 5 cups fresh fruit of your choice, such as strawberries, raspberries, kiwi fruit, bananas, grapes, peaches, pears, and orange sections
- Fresh lemon juice
- 2 cups apricot preserves

SUGAR-COATED ALMONDS

- 1 large egg white, at room temperature
- 1 tablespoon sugar
- 2 cups sliced blanched almonds, toasted

Make the dough: In a bowl or using a food processor, combine the flour, sugar, and egg yolks. Gradually add the melted butter and mix until the dough

Homegrown zinnias and petunias mixed with lacy herbs fill a commercial cookie jar from another era.

is smooth and gathers easily into a ball. Wrap the dough in plastic wrap and refrigerate for at least 1 hour.

Have ready a loose-bottomed tart pan or a springform pan.

On a lightly floured surface, roll out the dough to a ¼-inch thickness. Handling it as little as possible, fit the dough into the pan and flute the edges without attaching them firmly to the rim of the pan. Refrigerate the dough for 15 minutes. Preheat the oven to 350°F.

Bake the tart shell for 35 to 45 minutes, or until cooked through and lightly browned. If the pastry bubbles during baking, prick it lightly with the tines of a fork or the tip of a knife to deflate the bubbles; do not pierce the dough.

Set the tart shell aside on a wire rack to cool to room temperature.

Prepare the filling: Cut the fruit into manageable shapes and sizes, peeling when necessary, and coating those that will discolor with lemon juice.

In a nonstick saucepan, melt the apricot preserves. Strain through a fine

An almond-crusted mixed fruit tart made from an old German recipe is contributed by Lorraine and Charles Schmidt.

sieve and discard the solids.

Remove the tart shell from its baking pan and brush a thin coat of the apricot glaze over the bottom of the shell. Begin filling the tart with the fruit, arranging the slices decoratively and making a pleasing pattern of concentric rings or zigzags with different colors and types of fruits.

As each layer is completed, brush the fruit with apricot glaze to keep it in place and make it shiny.

Prepare the almonds: In a bowl, beat the egg white until it is frothy and soft peaks form. Continue beating, gradually adding the sugar, until stiff peaks form. Spread a thin coat of the beaten whites along the sides of the tart shell. One at a time or several at a time, firmly but carefully press the toasted almonds into the egg white to cover the outside of the tart completely.

Refrigerate the tart and serve in small wedges.

Serves 8 to 10

Butter-rich cinnamon-crumb topping makes Janell Edwards' apple pie a serious contender for all-time prize dessert.

CINNAMON-CRUMB-TOPPED APPLE PIE

If anything better exists on earth than Janell Edwards' custardy apple pie, topped with a mound of cinnamon crumbs, I haven't tasted it.

PIE

6 cups sliced, peeled baking apples, such as Golden Delicious or McIntosh (about 5 large apples)

1 9-inch unbaked deep-dish pie shell (see page 72)

1¼ cups granulated sugar

2 tablespoons cornstarch

4 tablespoons (½ stick) unsalted butter, melted and cooled

3 large egg yolks, beaten

½ cup heavy cream

¼ cup milk

Juice of ½ large lemon

CINNAMON-CRUMB TOPPING

11 tablespoons (1⅜ sticks) unsalted butter, softened

½ cup tightly packed light brown sugar

1⅔ cups all-purpose flour

1½ teaspoons ground cinnamon

Preheat the oven to 350°F.

Make the pie: Place the apples in the pie shell. In a large bowl or in a food processor, combine the granulated sugar, cornstarch, butter, and egg yolks. Mix until the sugar has dissolved. Add the cream, milk, and lemon juice and blend until smooth. Pour the filling over the apples and set aside.

Make the crumb topping: In a food processor or in a bowl, cream together the butter and brown sugar. Add the flour and cinnamon and process or stir until the mixture forms medium-size crumbs.

Evenly sprinkle the top of the pie with the crumbs and place the pie on a baking sheet. Bake for 1 hour to 1 hour and 10 minutes, or until the crumbs are lightly browned.

Place the pie on a wire rack to cool to room temperature and to allow the custard to set.

Cut into wedges and serve, accompanied by vanilla ice cream, if desired.

Serves 6 to 8

MENU

Tory's Gazpacho

Mesquite-Grilled Butterflied Leg of Lamb with Garlic Butter

Curried Mayonnaise

Deviled Eggs
page 54

Garden Tomatoes with Fresh Sweet Basil

Homemade Pickles

Dilly Bread

Lemon Squares
page 114

Iced Tea with Fresh Mint

Texas Hill Country

AIRPLANE PICNIC WITH THE CARTERS

In a big state, travel by air is a practical solution for meeting business needs and for socializing with close friends who are distant. Not surprisingly, the great state of Texas has more than its share of privately owned planes. And it leads the way in aircraft-style tailgating. Witness the efforts of Cheri and Bobby Carter as they fly from their Fredericksburg home to a business appointment in Egypt, Texas, and a chance to break bread with some old friends. Cheri's carry-on luggage is a picnic basket full of sophisticated Hill Country goodness.

The grassy field where Bob and Cheri Carter land their single-engine plane is easily made into a picnic ground.

TORY'S GAZPACHO

This tangy gazpacho is ideal for picnics. The recipe is a New Year's Day tradition at the home of the Carters' friend Tory Taylor.

3 tablespoons olive oil

⅓ cup chopped fresh mushrooms

1 garlic clove

2 teaspoons salt

2 cups minced ripe tomatoes

1¼ cups minced sweet green pepper

1 cup minced onions

1 cup diced celery

1 cup diced cucumber

1 tablespoon chopped fresh parsley

2 teaspoons snipped fresh chives

1 teaspoon freshly ground pepper

1 teaspoon Worcestershire sauce

¼ teaspoon hot pepper sauce or Tabasco

½ cup tarragon vinegar

2 cups canned tomato juice

2 cups chicken stock or broth

In a small skillet, warm the oil over moderate heat. Add the mushrooms and sauté until soft for 3 to 5 minutes.

In a large nonreactive bowl, crush the garlic with the salt. Add the mushrooms and all of the remaining ingredients. Stir well to combine.

Cover the soup and refrigerate for at least 3 hours or until well chilled. The gazpacho is better if made the night before you plan to serve it to allow time for the flavors to develop.

Serve cold in mugs with homemade croutons, if desired.

Serves 8 to 10

MESQUITE-GRILLED BUTTERFLIED LEG OF LAMB WITH GARLIC BUTTER

The meat is meltingly tender and moist when prepared this way over mesquite.

1 leg of lamb, butterflied (ask your butcher to do this)

MARINADE

1 12-ounce can beer

Juice of 1 large lemon

½ cup olive oil

6 large sprigs fresh rosemary, or 3 tablespoons dried

2 bay leaves, crumbled

3 garlic cloves, crushed

1 tablespoon sugar

½ cup soy sauce

2 teaspoons dry mustard

GARLIC BUTTER

¼ pound unsalted butter, at room temperature

2 garlic cloves, crushed or minced

Salt and freshly ground pepper

Trim away any unnecessary fat from the butterflied leg of lamb.

In a large bowl or nonaluminum pan, combine all of the marinade ingredients and mix well.

Place the lamb in the marinade and submerge as well as possible or turn to coat well with the marinade. Cover and refrigerate for 6 to 12 hours.

Prepare a grill, using mesquite or charcoal for fuel. When the coals are ash covered, drain the lamb and grill for 15 minutes. Turn the lamb and grill the other side for 15 minutes. The meat will be cooked medium-rare.

Meanwhile, make the garlic butter. In a small bowl, combine the butter, garlic, and salt and pepper to taste. As soon as it comes off the grill, brush the garlic butter all over the cooked lamb.

Thinly slice the lamb and serve hot, at room temperature, or cold.

Serves 8 to 12

CURRIED MAYONNAISE

Cheri Carter uses this versatile dip or spread for crudités, tomatoes, and grilled lamb and beef tenderloin.

1 cup mayonnaise, preferably homemade

1 tablespoon curry powder

1 tablespoon grated onion

1 garlic clove, finely minced

1 teaspoon tarragon vinegar

1 teaspoon prepared horseradish

In a bowl, combine all of the ingredients and mix well.

Cover and refrigerate until ready for use. If possible, make a day ahead of time to allow the flavors to develop. This dip will keep for 2 to 3 weeks.

Makes about 1 cup

On a rag rug, the picnic consists of marinated lamb, old-fashioned deviled eggs, gazpacho, and dilly bread (left). Mason jars of freshly brewed tea are brought to the site, then chilled with ice from a cooler. The Texas Hill Country includes vast expanses of open farmland (below left) as well as rocky terrain and man-made lakes.

GARDEN TOMATOES WITH FRESH SWEET BASIL

Peeling the tomatoes makes this salad an especially delicate treat.

4 large ripe tomatoes
⅓ to ½ cup virgin olive oil
Juice of 1 large lemon
Freshly ground pepper
4 to 6 large leaves fresh basil, chopped

In a pot of boiling water, submerge the tomatoes for 30 seconds. Cool under cold running water and peel off the skin. Cover and refrigerate.

Just before serving, slice the tomatoes. Drizzle with the olive oil and sprinkle with the lemon juice. Top with coarsely ground pepper and the chopped basil.

Serves 4

Note: You may substitute fresh dill, fennel, or chives for the basil, if desired.

DILLY BREAD

"Dilly Bread is great," says Cheri Carter, "you can do whatever you want to do with it—if you like onions, put in onions; if you like cheese, put in cheese." And if you add nothing extra at all, I think you'll like it just as it is.

1 package active dry yeast
2 tablespoons sugar
¼ cup lukewarm water (105° to 115°F.)
1 cup creamy cottage cheese
1 tablespoon snipped fresh chives
1 tablespoon unsalted butter, melted
4 large sprigs fresh dill, minced, or 2 teaspoons dill seed
1 teaspoon salt
¼ teaspoon baking soda
1 egg, beaten
2¼ to 2½ cups all-purpose flour
Melted butter and salt, for the top of the baked loaf

In a cup or small bowl, stir the yeast and sugar into the warm water until dissolved. Set aside to proof for about 10 minutes, or until frothy.

In a small saucepan, place the cottage cheese over low heat and cook just until lukewarm; if too hot, it could kill the yeast.

In a large bowl, combine the yeast, cottage cheese, chives, butter, dill, salt, baking soda, and egg. Add the flour and stir until the mixture forms a soft, somewhat sticky dough.

Lightly oil a clean bowl and turn the dough into it. Cover and set aside to rise in a draft-free place until double in size, about 1 hour.

Grease an 8-inch round casserole. Stir down the dough and turn into the casserole. Cover and let rise again until light and almost double, about 1 hour.

Preheat the oven to 350°F. Bake the bread in the center of the oven for 40 to 50 minutes, until it is lightly browned on top and the bottom sounds hollow when tapped. Brush the top of the loaf with melted butter and sprinkle with salt while still hot. Let cool to room temperature.

Makes one 8-inch loaf

MENU

Open-Faced Herb Tea Sandwiches

Cream Cheese, Olive, and Walnut Tea Sandwiches

Favorite Old-Fashioned Brown Sugar Sandwiches

Cheese Platter

Homemade Bread

Sardines

Lemon Shortbread

Tart Lemon Squares

Chocolate-Raspberry Pound Cake

Fresh Strawberries with Thick Cream

Watermelon

Clusters of Red and Green Grapes

Iced Peppermint Sun Tea

Bottled Sparkling Apple Cider

COUNTRY TEA PARTY
AT CYNTHIA
PEDREGON'S

Texas Hill Country

Teatime— that most pleasant late-afternoon ritual that came to the Colonies with the English—is a chance to bring out the fine silver, crisp linens, and bone china, and enjoy a light meal to bridge the gap between lunch and dinner.

A Texas-style tea party has all these elements but with a regional twist. After a day of antiquing in the Hill Country of Texas, I had the chance to experience one.

We were at a country retreat near Fredericksburg, the nineteenth-century community of six thousand residents, with a German heritage as solid as its limestone-chinked *fachwerk* houses. It was here, in the shade of a tree, that Cynthia Pedregon and her friends introduced me to the pleasure of sipping iced tea and munching brown sugar sandwiches.

Cynthia's Texas interpretation of the event came naturally. She owns and op-

A Country tea table is flanked by Carol Bade, left, and Cynthia Pedregon, right. Joan Harris wears a lace-trimmed apron. Ottis Layne holds fiddle, and wife, Sally, baby Anna.

erates the Peach Tree Gift Gallery in Fredericksburg, which sells the wares of local artists and craftsmen and also includes a busy tearoom. The shop offers a daily changing selection of freshly made soups and entrées, delicately flavored with herbs, and stresses seasonal dishes like asparagus quiche in the spring and ice-cream pie with orchard peaches in the summer.

At the alfresco tea, instead of sitting at tea tables in overstuffed wing chairs, we pulled twig chairs up to rustic pine and oak tables. Colorful quilts served as our tablecloths. Wooden bowls and pewter pitchers replaced the fine English and French china and porcelain. And, most important, instead of hot tea, we had iced tea garnished with pineapple stalks, mint leaves, and fluted orange slices. If Texas were still a republic, iced tea would surely be its national beverage; true Texans swear by it in their struggle with heat and humidity.

Exchanging intimate bits of gossip and other social notes is another time-honored part of the tea party ritual, and the simple country furniture, hand-crafts, fresh flowers, and impromptu fiddle playing (by friend Ottis Layne) provided the right setting. "I like get-togethers that are unpretentious," notes Cynthia. "Our home entertaining tends to be spontaneous—we'll invite friends over for Mexican food and spend the evening renewing our acquaintance around the supper table."

Cynthia has had a lifelong interest in preparing and serving foods well. "When I was growing up, my mother helped out in the family business," Cynthia relates. "She also loved to garden, so we made a deal. I did the cooking and she tended her flowers."

As a teen-ager, Cynthia worked in the employee snack bar in her folks' Medina, Texas, factory. "I learned to make exotic items like egg rolls and lots of standard casseroles," she says. But her most important culinary influence was her favorite aunt, Jo Collins.

"Aunt Jo came to visit frequently and always brought her recipe notebooks with her," Cynthia recalls. "She really taught me the fine points of cooking, as we worked side by side in the kitchen, trying out new recipes and improvising on old ones. I still serve specialties like her delicious herb sandwiches in the tearoom today."

OPEN-FACED HERB TEA SANDWICHES

No tea party would be complete without little sandwiches with flavorful fillings. You can vary the herbs for this spread by adding or substituting small amounts of fresh thyme, oregano, or tarragon.

> 4 cups parsley sprigs
> 2 tablespoons chopped onion
> 1 tablespoon fresh basil leaves, or
>   1 teaspoon dried basil
> ¾ to 1 cup mayonnaise, preferably
>   homemade
>   Salt and freshly ground black pepper
> 1 loaf thin-sliced bread
>   Softened unsalted butter for the bread

In a food processor fitted with a metal blade, combine the parsley, onion, and basil. Process until very finely chopped.

Remove to a small bowl and stir in the mayonnaise. Season with salt and pepper to taste.

Cover and refrigerate for several hours or overnight.

Trim the crusts from the bread. Lightly butter one side of each slice. Spread the herb filling on each slice and cut the slices into triangles before serving. (If not serving immediately, wrap the sandwiches in a damp tea towel or in dampened paper towels to prevent them from drying out.)

Serves 8 to 10

Pewter pitchers filled with freshly brewed peppermint tea are kept on ice in a copper tub.

An old wire basket is a countrified version of an ice bucket.

CREAM CHEESE, OLIVE, AND WALNUT TEA SANDWICHES

If not using the filling immediately, cover and refrigerate it. When ready to use, let the filling come to room temperature before spreading it on the bread slices. The bread will tear if the mixture is too firm.

> 1 8-ounce package cream cheese,
>   softened
> ⅓ cup finely chopped green and black
>   olives
> ¼ cup finely chopped walnuts
> 2 tablespoons chopped fresh parsley
> 1 loaf thin-sliced whole wheat bread

In a bowl or with a food processor, beat the cream cheese until light and fluffy. Add the olives, walnuts, and parsley and mix together.

Trim the crusts from the bread. Spread half the slices with the filling and cover with the remaining bread slices. Cut the sandwiches into triangles and serve.

Serves 8 to 10

FAVORITE OLD-FASHIONED BROWN SUGAR SANDWICHES

Cynthia Pedregon's father pioneered these sandwiches, which have become a family tradition.

1 loaf thin-sliced bread
  Softened unsalted butter
  Soft dark brown sugar

Trim the crusts from the bread. Lightly butter the slices and coat half of the slices with a thin layer of brown sugar. Top with slices of bread and cut into triangles.

Wrap the sandwiches tightly in plastic wrap for no more than 1 to 2 hours before serving.

Serves 8 to 10

A tangy alternative to the menu of sweets, this selection of cheeses and homemade breads is presented on a flowery chintz spread.

Lemon Shortbread

Sally Layne's mother makes the shortbread plain, without the lemon, and spreads it very thin over a jelly roll pan so she can use it as a shortbread base for fresh strawberries and ice cream. Sally's family enjoys this version for their afternoon tea.

1 pound (4 sticks) unsalted butter,
    softened
1 scant cup sugar (1 cup less
    1 tablespoon)
1 tablespoon lemon extract
    About 5 cups all-purpose flour
    Sugar or granulated maple sugar for
    dusting the baked shortbread

Preheat the oven to 350°F.

In a bowl, use an electric mixer to cream together the butter, sugar, and lemon extract until fluffy; the mixture should not be grainy to the touch.

One cup at a time, add the flour and beat thoroughly. If the dough feels moist, add up to 1 cup more flour, until the dough is firm but not dry.

Using the fingers, evenly pat the dough into a 13 x 9 x 2-inch glass baking dish. Press down on the dough with the back of a fork. Bake in the center of the oven for 15 minutes.

Remove the shortbread from the oven and press down again with the back of a fork. Return to the oven and bake for 20 to 25 minutes more, or until the edges are lightly browned.

Remove the pan to a wire rack and sprinkle the shortbread with sugar. Cut into squares while hot. Let cool to room temperature and serve or store in an airtight container for up to 1 week.

To make shaped shortbread cookies, proceed as follows:

Prepare the dough and wrap well in plastic wrap. Chill for at least 2 hours. (The dough can be made a day ahead of time.)

Working quickly to keep the dough from warming up, roll out the dough to a ¼- to ½-inch thickness. Press the dough into molds or cut with shaped cookie cutters. Using a spatula, place cookies about 1 inch apart on an un-greased baking sheet. Bake at 350°F., until lightly browned around the edges, 10 to 15 minutes.

Makes about 2 dozen squares or shaped cookies

Tart Lemon Squares

Carol Bade's lemon squares are just right for anyone who loves tart flavors.

6 tablespoons (¾ stick) unsalted butter,
    softened
¼ cup confectioners' sugar
1 cup plus 3 tablespoons all-purpose
    flour
3 large eggs
1 cup granulated sugar
¼ cup fresh lemon juice
    Grated rind of ½ lemon
    Confectioners' sugar for dusting

Preheat the oven to 350°F.

In a food processor or with an electric mixer, cream the butter, confectioners' sugar, and 1 cup of the flour.

Gently pat the dough into a 9-inch square baking pan. Bake for 15 minutes, or until lightly browned.

Meanwhile, in a bowl, lightly beat the eggs. Mix together the granulated sugar and the remaining 3 tablespoons of flour and add them to the eggs. Stir in the lemon juice and lemon rind.

When the crust has baked for 15 minutes, remove the pan from the oven and pour the lemon mixture on top. Bake for 15 to 20 minutes, or until the mixture appears to be firm.

Remove the pan to a wire rack and dust lightly while still hot with confectioners' sugar. Use a spatula to loosen the edges from the sides of the pan and allow to cool to room temperature. Cut into 1½-inch squares and serve.

Makes 3 dozen

Chocolate-Raspberry Pound Cake

Juli Dodds makes this pound cake all the time— and coats the layers with pineapple, apricot, or just chocolate—whatever appeals that day.

1 16-ounce store-bought frozen pound
    cake
1½ cups raspberry jam
1 12-ounce package semisweet
    chocolate chips (2 cups)
1 cup sour cream
1 teaspoon vanilla extract
2 teaspoons framboise, kirsch, or
    Mandarine liqueur (optional)

While the pound cake is still frozen, use a serrated knife to slice it horizontally into five or six thin layers. (This is more difficult with a thawed cake.)

Generously coat each cake layer with the raspberry jam, stacking the layers evenly on top of one another.

In a double boiler over hot water, melt the chocolate chips with the sour

cream. Remove from the heat and stir in the vanilla. If desired, stir in the liqueur.

Reserving ⅔ cup of the frosting, spread the chocolate while still warm over the top and sides of the cake. Refrigerate.

Just before serving, fit a pastry bag with a decorative tip and fill with the cooled chocolate mixture. Pipe decorations on the top and sides of the cake.

Serves 8 to 10

ICED PEPPERMINT SUN TEA

Sally Layne makes this tea from mint leaves she harvests every fall. "Each year, when the bloom is at its height, we cut the peppermint that has taken over the bank of our creek. We hang it in a cool, dark closet until dry, and then we store it in old blue glass battery jars. It has kept us supplied with peppermint tea for the last six years."

About ½ cup dried peppermint leaves
Mint sprigs for garnish

Put the peppermint leaves in a gallon jar. Add 1 gallon of water and cover. Set outside, directly in the sun, for 3 to 5 hours.

Serve over ice and garnish with sprigs of fresh mint.

Makes 1 gallon

Fancy family silver and lacy linens mix with simple trays, baskets, and boards for serving up sugar-coated cookies and chocolate iced cake at a down-home version of afternoon tea.

Fredericksburg, Texas

In front of a stone house built by German immigrants in the late 1880s, the table is laid for a buffet dinner with checkered cloth and napkins and Country plates and platters (right).
Chile peppers hung to dry are a sample of the hundreds of vegetables, flowers, and herbs grown by Lynn and Don Watt (below) at their River Bend Farm.

Improvising a successful meal out of what happens to be available in the garden is a daily routine on the fertile River Bend Farm of Lynn and Don Watt in the scenic Hill Country of Texas. "I was strictly a chicken-on-the-grill kind of cook until I met Lynn," Don admits. "Now we improvise and create, letting the best things in the garden on any given day dictate our menu."

As is the custom in Texas whenever a newcomer comes to town, it's a ready excuse for a spontaneous gathering such as the homegrown farm dinner the Watts prepared for me. On the day I visited, freshly gathered sweet basil, opal basil, thyme, and Italian parsley provided the inspiration for the evening meal, a classic beef tenderloin with Madeira sauce.

"We're very easygoing," says Lynn about the Watts' style of entertaining. "Usually we just call up friends at four and say, 'Why don't y'all come over around seven?'" Whether the meal is beef, fish, pasta, or chicken, it's always enlivened with one or more of the many varieties of herbs growing a short walk from the house. Guests tag along on these forays, then make themselves comfortable in the kitchen while the food is being prepared.

Lynn's interest in raising culinary herbs led to the couple's moving to River Bend four years ago. The property, so named because it hugs the bend in the Pedernales River, is in an area not far from Fredericksburg that was first settled over a century ago by German immigrants. A stone barn, built in 1878, features narrow "Indian-proof" windows—to protect frontiersmen against surprise visits. The two-story stone house, dating from 1880, was considered a "tear-down" item by the real estate agent who showed it, but the Watts saw the potential in its pine floors, wood-beamed ceilings, and spacious kitchen. They saved the structure with an eight-month renovation effort and created an authentic country home.

Tall mesquite trees on the site provide shade and aromatic fuel for outdoor cooking. There are also peach trees and apple trees (both fruits are grown commercially in the region). Don plants a ¾-acre garden with a wide range of vegetables and smaller gardens with over seventy varieties of herbs, most of them for the kitchen. Statice and strawflower are grown in volume for fresh and dried bouquets.

MENU

Texas-Style Fish Pâté

*Herb–Cheddar Cheese
Spread*

*Garden-Fresh Sliced
Tomatoes with Mozzarella
and Basil on a Bed of
Arugula*

*Beef Tenderloin with
Madeira Sauce*

*Chicken Salad with Pasta
and Herbs*

*French Bread with Herb
Butter*

Assorted Cookies

Shiner Bock Beer

*Sutter Home White
Zinfandel*

Bundles of statice, starflowers, and herbs are hung to dry in the stone barn with its original Indian-proof windows and the household's No. 1 catnip fancier (left). Blackboard specials at the barnside stand (right) include fresh-cut herbs, fruit, and vegetables.

Interestingly, the noted German portraitist Friedrich Richard Petri and landscape painter Hermann Lungkwitz lived and worked in cabins on the site of River Bend Farm during the 1850s, painting in the Romantic tradition which documented much of the American West.

In their own way the Watts have a similar vision of country life. They are latter-day Romantics who keep the values and traditions of River Bend intact.

TEXAS-STYLE FISH PÂTÉ

Don Watt created this classic fish pâté with regional ingredients, such as catfish and nopalitos.

> 2 large sweet red peppers, or 1 sweet red pepper and 2 to 3 mild red jalapeño peppers
> 2 pounds catfish, redfish, or red snapper fillets
> 2 large eggs, lightly beaten
> ½ cup heavy cream
>   Dash of Tabasco sauce
>   Salt and freshly ground black pepper
> ½ cup dry white wine
> ¼ cup minced fresh cilantro (coriander)
> ½ cup minced Italian flat-leaf parsley
> ¾ to 1 cup canned nopalitos (cactus leaves, cut into strips, available at some specialty food stores)

Preheat the oven to 325°F. Butter an 8 x 4-inch terrine. Seed, devein, and finely chop the sweet red peppers. Put them in a strainer to drain.

Using a food processor fitted with a metal blade, mince the fish fillets. Add the eggs, cream, Tabasco sauce, and salt and pepper to taste and process to combine. A little at a time, add the wine and process until the purée is thick and smooth.

Layer one-third of the fish purée into the buttered terrine. Mix together the cilantro and parsley and sprinkle evenly over the fish to make a green layer. Carefully layer half of the remaining fish purée over the herbs and smooth the top. Add a crosswise layer of chopped pepper and place strips of nopalitos lengthwise over the peppers. Smooth the remaining purée on top.

Cover with aluminum foil and the terrine lid. Place the terrine in a baking dish and add warm water to reach halfway up the side of the terrine. Bake for 1½ to 2 hours, or until a metal skewer inserted in the center comes out clean.

Drain off excess liquid and let the pâté come to room temperature. Let flavors develop in refrigerator overnight. Cut into thin slices and serve chilled.

Serves 12 to 16

HERB–CHEDDAR
CHEESE SPREAD

8 to 10 sprigs Italian flat-leaf parsley

1 tablespoon fresh thyme leaves

1½ teaspoons fresh oregano, or ½
    teaspoon dried oregano

½ teaspoon freshly ground white pepper

1 8-ounce package cream cheese,
    softened

8 tablespoons (1 stick) unsalted butter,
    softened

1 pound mild Cheddar cheese,
    shredded

    Sweet red pepper julienne and parsley
    and thyme leaves for decoration

Crusty French bread

In a food processor, combine the parsley, thyme, oregano, and white pepper. Process until finely chopped. Add the cream cheese and butter and process until smooth, about 1 minute. Add the Cheddar cheese and process until the mixture is thoroughly combined.

Found objects make effective building materials: cedar posts from the ruins of a cistern edge the flower garden; flat rocks collected from the Pedernales River form the walkway from house to barn.

Turn the cheese spread into a decorative mold or shape into a ball with your fingers. Cover and chill for about 30 minutes before serving.

Let the spread come to room temperature and decorate with red pepper julienne and herb leaves. Accompany with crusty French bread.

Serves 12 to 16

BEEF TENDERLOIN
WITH MADEIRA SAUCE

If you want to grill this tenderloin outside, over mesquite, the Madeira sauce will benefit from a flavorful beef stock since the pan juices won't add to the flavor.

2 garlic cloves

2 tablespoons unsalted butter, softened

1 tablespoon chopped fresh thyme

1 4- to 5-pound beef tenderloin

½ cup Madeira

1 cup beef stock or broth

2 tablespoons all-purpose flour blended
    with 2 tablespoons softened unsalted
    butter (beurre manié)

Salt and freshly ground black pepper

This homegrown menu has a distinct herbal accent, featuring tomatoes with basil and mozzarella, Cheddar cheese spread fortified with oregano and thyme, grilled beef tenderloin seasoned with chopped thyme, chicken pasta salad with parsley, thyme, and two varieties of basil, and fish pâté layered with minced parsley and cilantro.

Preheat the oven to 400°F. Crush or finely mince the garlic and blend well with the butter and thyme. Rub the mixture all over the meat.

Folding the thin end of the fillet under, place the beef in a roasting pan, and roast for 20 to 35 minutes, or until a meat thermometer registers 120°F. for rare or higher for more well-done meat.

Remove the beef to a platter and cover with aluminum foil to keep it warm. Place the roasting pan on the stove top and add the Madeira and beef stock. Deglaze the pan over moderately high heat, scraping up the brown bits that cling to the bottom, and cook until the sauce is reduced by half, 6 to 8 minutes. Turn the heat to moderately low, stir in the flour and butter mixture to thicken the sauce, and simmer for 8 to 10 minutes to cook the flour. Taste and season with salt and pepper. Serve the sauce over warm sliced beef.

Serves 12 to 16

Chicken Salad with Pasta and Herbs

This perfect combination of chicken and pasta produces a light, stylish-looking salad.

RIVER BEND VINAIGRETTE

- 2 large egg yolks, at room temperature
- 2 tablespoons Dijon mustard
- 1 cup vegetable oil
- ⅔ cup olive oil
- ¼ cup basil vinegar (fresh basil leaves steeped in white wine vinegar)
- Salt and freshly ground black pepper
- About ½ cup lukewarm water

SALAD

- 2 whole poached chicken breasts
- 1 pound fettuccine, preferably fresh or homemade
- ½ pound snow pea pods, trimmed
- ½ pound asparagus spears
- 1 large sweet red pepper, seeded and cut into fine julienne
- 12 cherry tomatoes, halved and drained
- ½ cup chopped fresh sweet basil
- ¼ cup chopped fresh dark opal basil
- ¼ cup chopped fresh Italian flat-leaf parsley
- 1 tablespoon chopped fresh thyme
- Salt and freshly ground black pepper

Make the vinaigrette: In a blender or food processor fitted with a metal blade, combine the egg yolks and mustard. With the motor running, add the vegetable and olive oils in a thin stream. Process until well emulsified. Add the vinegar and salt and pepper to taste and thin to a coating consistency with the lukewarm water. Set aside.

Make the salad: Put a large pot of water on the stove to boil for the pasta. Meanwhile, pull the chicken off the bones and shred or dice it. Set it aside.

Cook the fettuccine until just *al dente*. Drain and turn into a large bowl. Add the chicken and vinaigrette and toss to coat well. Set aside.

Blanch the snow peas in boiling water for 30 seconds. Refresh under cold running water and turn into a strainer to drain.

Bend each asparagus spear until it snaps. Reserve the stems for another use or discard them; steam the tips until crisp-tender, 1 to 3 minutes, depending on size. Refresh under cold running water and drain.

Add the snow peas, asparagus spears, sweet red pepper julienne, cherry tomatoes, basils, parsley, and thyme to the chicken and pasta and toss to coat with the dressing and distribute evenly. Season with salt and pepper to taste. Serve at room temperature or cover and refrigerate for up to 3 days.

Serves 10 to 12

Herb Butter

You'll want to make a large quantity so that there's always some flavored butter on hand—not just for spreading on bread, but for scrambled eggs, sautéed chicken, and broiled fish.

- ½ pound (2 sticks) unsalted butter, softened
- ½ cup minced fresh basil leaves, 3 tablespoons minced fresh tarragon, or ¼ cup minced chives

Using a food processor or a bowl and spoon, combine the butter with one of the herbs, mixing very well. When thoroughly blended, spoon the mixture into a ramekin or shape into logs and wrap in plastic wrap.

Chill for at least 1 hour to allow the flavors to develop.

Makes ½ pound

Two bountiful fall crops, red chile
peppers and crookneck squash
(above), await a kitchen solution.
Herbs and vegetables are used to
trim the house (above left). A clay
pot (right) makes an outdoor sink.

Houston, Texas

MEXICAN BUFFET BY THE POOL AT CAROL LEVERETT'S

Poolside entertaining in Houston, under an Italian market umbrella (above), evokes the open-air tradition of life South of the Border, where food is often prepared, served, and savored out of doors.

At about the time northerners are putting their own pools to bed, poolside entertaining in Houston, Texas, comes into its own. Summer weather conditions extend well into the fall in this area, as I discovered one sweltering September day when I was in town for a book signing. Carol Leverett came to my rescue by inviting me to her Georgian-style house in River Oaks for a Tex-Mex banquet served alfresco on her spacious wood deck.

Carol's West Texas roots are evident in the home-cooked specialties she likes to treat her guests to. "I grew up with Mexican housekeepers who regularly prepared their native dishes for our family, and I've never lost my enthusiasm for this cuisine."

On this day Carol served flour tortillas, *fajitas* (marinated flank steak), guacamole, salsa, and sour cream Country style with her collection of English stoneware bowls and platters and colorful Mexican pottery. This help-yourself style of dining always puts guests at ease and encourages conversation.

"It also travels well," Carol declares. An interior designer, she makes frequent trips to London in search of En-glish accessories for her antiques shop, Carol Leverett Interiors & Antiques, in Houston, and on one such trip she filled a canvas carry-on with all the ingredients necessary to treat an expatriate friend to a Tex-Mex feast.

At home, Carol's casual approach to entertaining is evident in the flower arrangements she improvises out of roses plucked from her garden and her standing invitation to friends to join her in her lacquered red kitchen as she prepares the meal.

"With everyone so busy these days, there's not that much time for planning elaborate social affairs," she notes, remembering with a laugh her young married days when she dutifully followed the dictates of Julia Child. "Five-course dinners were standard operating procedure," she recalls. "And I wouldn't dare serve a new menu without trying it out earlier in the week!" Today, Carol may host a formal dinner only once or twice a year. "My ideas for entertaining have changed dramatically," she says, reflecting the experience many of us have today. "Now, simple food, beautifully presented, is what really interests me."

M E N U

Guacamole

Fajitas

Chile con Queso

Pico de Gallo

Mexican Rice

Pralines

Ice-Cold Beer

Red Wine

◇◆◇◆◇◆◇

*A crisp cotton cloth
transforms the built-in deck
bench into a buffet table.
The serve-yourself buffet of
fajitas with traditional
condiments, including ice-cold
beer, is offered in English
stoneware and Mexican bowls.*

GUACAMOLE

1 medium onion, minced
Juice of ½ lemon
3 tablespoons fresh or canned jalapeño
pepper
5 large ripe avocados, peeled and diced
Salt

In a bowl, combine the onion, lemon juice, and jalapeño pepper. Stir in avocado well. Season with salt to taste. Turn the guacamole into a bowl and serve immediately at room temperature, with tortilla chips.

Serves 6 to 8

FAJITAS

About 6 pounds beef skirt steak or
flank steak, trimmed well (If using
thick skirt steak, cut in half
horizontally.)
½ cup vegetable oil
¾ cup beer, at room temperature
Juice of 2 lemons or limes
1 tablespoon soy sauce
1 teaspoon ground cumin
Salt and freshly ground black pepper
Lime slices for garnish
2 dozen extra-large flour tortillas, heated
until soft, for serving

Let the meat come to room temperature. In a bowl or nonreactive pan, combine the oil, beer, lemon juice, soy sauce, cumin, and salt and pepper to taste. Add the steak and marinate at room temperature, turning several times, for at least 4 hours, or cover and refrigerate overnight.

Prepare a grill with plenty of charcoal. When the coals are ash covered and glowing, sear the steak, turning it when the flames rise, for 10 minutes.

Remove the steak to a cutting board and slice it thinly crosswise into ¼-inch strips. Wrap the meat and juices in a double thickness of foil and return the package to the grill for 20 minutes.

Serve the fajitas hot, accompanied by Pico de Gallo, Guacamole, Chile con Queso, and warm tortillas.

Serves 6 to 8

CHILE CON QUESO

This is delicious with fajitas, with corn chips, steamed vegetables, or even a BLT.

2 tablespoons unsalted butter
1 onion, minced
1 16-ounce can Rotel tomatoes, if
available in your area, or 1 can
Italian plum tomatoes mixed with
2 tablespoons chopped hot red chile
pepper and ½ teaspoon dried oregano
1 32-ounce package Velveeta cheese, or
1 cup grated Cheddar cheese, 1 cup
grated Monterey Jack cheese, and
1 3-ounce package cream cheese

In a large saucepan, melt the butter over moderate heat. Add the onion and sauté until soft, 3 to 5 minutes. Stir in the tomatoes and cook for 5 minutes.

Cube the cheese and add it to the tomato mixture. Cook, stirring frequently, until melted. Keep the chile warm for serving, or refrigerate and reheat.

Serves 6 to 8

PICO DE GALLO

2 large ripe tomatoes, peeled and
chopped
1 large onion, chopped
1 fresh jalapeño pepper, seeded and
minced
Juice of 2 limes
Salt and freshly ground black pepper
¼ cup minced fresh cilantro (coriander)

In a bowl, combine the tomatoes, onion, and jalapeño pepper. Add the lime juice and salt and pepper to taste. Sprinkle with the cilantro and toss. Cover and refrigerate until 30 minutes before serving at room temperature with grilled beef or chips.

Serves 6 to 8

MEXICAN RICE

¼ cup vegetable oil
1 cup white rice
1 8-ounce can tomato sauce
½ cup minced onion
1 garlic clove, halved
Salt (optional)
Sliced sweet green peppers for garnish

In a saucepan, warm the oil over moderate heat. Add the rice and sauté until golden, 2 to 3 minutes. Remove from the heat. In a blender or food processor, purée the tomato sauce,

Antique Staffordshire plates mix with hand-blown Mexican glasses. Wicker-covered bottles contain Tabasco sauce, lime juice, and salsa.

onion, and garlic until smooth.

Pour the tomato purée over the rice and add 2 cups of water. Season with salt to taste. Bring the mixture to a boil over high heat, cover, and turn heat to low. Simmer for 25 minutes, or until water evaporates. Serve hot, garnished with green peppers.

Serves 6 to 8

PRALINES

This traditional southern sweet treat is a soothing finish to a highly spiced meal.

  3 cups sugar
1½ cups buttermilk
  1 teaspoon baking soda
    Pinch of salt
  4 tablespoons (½ stick) unsalted butter
  2 cups pecan halves or pieces
  1 teaspoon vanilla extract

In a large heavy saucepan, combine the sugar, buttermilk, baking soda, and salt. Bring to a boil over moderately high heat and add the butter, a little at a time. Stir in the pecans.

Place a candy thermometer in the pan and cook until the mixture reaches the soft-ball stage and the thermometer reads 234° to 240°F.

Remove from the heat and stir in the vanilla. Beat briskly with a wooden spoon until the mixture is cool and stiff. Drop by tablespoons onto wax paper and let harden before serving or storing in an airtight container.

Makes about 2 dozen

In a hub-of-the-house Country kitchen, this Texas-style smorgasbord of ribs and brisket is presented on an antique English butcher block countertop.

M E N U

Barbecued Brisket and Ribs

Tommy Jacomini's Barbecue Sauce for Brisket and Ribs

Cheese Grits with Jalapeños

Three-Bean Salad

Buttermilk Pie

☆☆☆☆☆

TEXAS BARBECUE AT BEVERLY AND TOMMY JACOMINI'S

☆☆☆☆☆

Houston, Texas

Nothing says "Texas" to me more eloquently than pit-cooked barbecue—especially when the pit is two feet deep by thirty-five feet long and equipped with a firebox full of ready-to-burn hickory and mesquite. The barbecue pit I speak of runs along the side of the elegant Georgian-style Houston house that belongs to Beverly and Tommy Jacomini.

I was researching my first book when I met the Jacominis more than ten years ago. Beverly is an accomplished interior designer, and we became fast friends, in part because of our similar tastes and love of the Country look. I can remember calling Bev up shortly after that first meeting and saying, "You have one of everything I have!" Tommy is a successful restaurateur, operating the legendary Hofbrau in Houston, where people flock for the premium steaks, ice-cold beer in "long-neck" bottles, and raucous and sentimental country-western music on the house jukebox.

Beverly enjoys teasing me about the circumstances of our meeting. It was midsummer, the daily temperatures hovered around 100°F., and I was trekking across Texas in boots and layers of skirts. Beverly invited me to take a weekend break at her farmhouse, and there she kindly pointed out to me that all the real cowgirls that summer were wearing shorts and sandals.

The Hill Country farmhouse has been the inspiration for Beverly's entertaining style. "The farm has taught me how to do beautiful things simply," she says, like presenting dishes on well-worn cutting boards or mixing elegant silver with copper or heaping bunches of fresh flowers into Country pitchers and bowls.

From the start, the kitchen in Houston was important to Beverly and Tommy's social plans. "We remodeled it to become the hub of the home," Beverly recalls. "We wanted a kitchen that you didn't close the door on." New oak cabinets were built and treated to look like old English pine. A genuine antique slab of English butcher block was installed to serve as a buffet. "Now the kitchen makes it possible to have a dinner party without insisting on formality," says Beverly. "But it doesn't exclude formality, either; we've had black-tie buffets complete with silver

and linen before occasions like the ballet, and the space works for that just as well as for down-home barbecue."

Beverly grew up in a family that included five daughters, "so there was always something doing in the kitchen," she recalls. She still falls back on the tried and true recipes and canning and pickling techniques she learned as a child, and the farm has enabled her to recapture the warm atmosphere she enjoyed while growing up. "Eating in our kitchen, whether in the city or at the farm, helps to keep things down home,"

Both avid cooks, Beverly and Tommy Jacomini make frequent use of the professional range and other equipment in their kitchen. The copper pots are hung from hooks that originally hoisted mailbags on the railroad in Great Britain.

A scrubbed pine table, flanked by Windsor-style chairs, makes the kitchen the place of choice for family meals. The Spode china plates, everyday tableware for middle-class English households in the 19th century, have piecrust edging.

she notes. "When you offer good food in a comfortable setting, everyone looks forward to coming to dinner."

And if you're going to a barbecue in the summer, at least in Texas, don't be afraid to come in shorts.

☆☆☆☆☆

BARBECUED BRISKET AND RIBS

To make "real barbecue"—Texas style—you need a dug-in-the-ground barbecue pit, a large quantity of meat, and time. The Jacominis' pit is 35 feet long, with the firebox set off to the side. Tommy uses hickory or mesquite to fuel the fire and can adjust the flue to regulate the amount of heat that gets into the pit.

Start with at least 60 pounds of pork spareribs and a 10-pound beef brisket. In a large tub, mix together 1 part vegetable oil, 3 parts cider or wine vinegar, 1 part brown sugar, and lots of chopped onion to make a marinade for the ribs. Marinate for 8 hours or overnight. To cook the ribs, burn wood in the firebox until the pit temperature reaches 300°F. Add the ribs and barbecue, with the pit covered, for about 4 hours, or until they are very tender. Serve hot, with Tommy's barbecue sauce.

To cook the brisket, season it with salt and pepper and place the brisket in the pit at the opposite end from the fire. Cover the pit and cook over *very low* heat for 6 to 7 hours. As the brisket cooks, the meat will turn brown. It is perfectly done when the "smoke ring," the pink rim, moves from the center of the meat out to the edge and is only about ¼ inch thick. If the heat is too high, the ring will not develop properly. If the brisket is not tender enough after 6 to 7 hours, wrap it in aluminum foil and set it on the grill. Cover the pit and let cook 30 to 40 minutes more, or until it is very tender. Serve hot with Tommy's barbecue sauce.

☆☆☆☆☆

TOMMY JACOMINI'S BARBECUE SAUCE FOR BRISKET AND RIBS

This sauce has so many layers of good flavor that it almost tastes different every time you use it. Remember, it's not for marinating or basting, but to accompany meat.

2 medium onions, quartered
1 large ripe tomato, quartered
3 garlic cloves
1 jalapeño pepper, seeded and quartered
½ cup fresh cilantro (coriander) leaves
1 14-ounce can Rotel tomatoes, if available in your area, or Italian plum tomatoes
1 cup firmly packed light brown sugar
2 cups ketchup
 Juice of 1 lemon
2 tablespoons Worcestershire sauce
1 tablespoon prepared horseradish
1 tablespoon prepared mustard
1 tablespoon A-1 Sauce
 Pinch of dried oregano
 Pinch of dried thyme
1 12-ounce can beer

In a food processor fitted with a metal blade, combine the onions, to- mato, garlic, jalapeño, and cilantro. Process until finely chopped.

If your food processor has a capacity of 12 cups, add all of the remaining sauce ingredients and process until completely puréed. If the capacity is smaller than 12 cups, add the canned tomatoes and brown sugar and process until finely puréed. Turn the purée into a large bowl and stir in the remaining ingredients.

Refrigerate the sauce, covered, and let come to room temperature before serving. The sauce will keep up to 1 week in the refrigerator.

Makes 3 quarts

☆☆☆☆☆

B. JACOMINI

Tommy, a Houston restaurateur, rustles up sausages and ribs on a home cooker.

CHEESE GRITS WITH JALAPEÑOS

The grits are a perfect foil for the flavors of the jalapeño and sharp Cheddar cheese and the texture is soft and smooth—not gritslike at all.

1½ cups quick (not instant) grits
1 pound sharp Cheddar cheese,
    shredded (about 5 cups)
3 large eggs, beaten
6 tablespoons (¾ stick) unsalted butter,
    melted
1 mild fresh or canned jalapeño
    pepper, seeded and chopped
2 teaspoons salt
    Dash of Tabasco sauce

Preheat the oven to 250°F. Oil or butter a 1½- to 2-quart casserole.

In a medium heavy saucepan, bring 6 cups of water to a boil over high heat. Add the grits and turn the heat to moderately low. Cook, stirring, until the grits are very thick, about 4 minutes.

Remove from the heat and stir in the cheese, eggs, melted butter, jalapeño, salt, and Tabasco sauce.

Turn the grits into the prepared casserole and bake for 1 hour, or until the top is golden. Serve hot.

Serves 8 to 10

⭒⭒⭒⭒⭒

An antique English pine plate holder stores a collection of platters and old cutting boards.

THREE-BEAN SALAD

Here's a cooling, flavorful bean-and-vegetable salad that can be served year-round.

1 pound fresh green and/or waxed
    beans, blanched, trimmed, and cut
    into 1½-inch pieces
2 15-ounce cans kidney beans, drained
1½ cups diced celery
1 pound fresh mushrooms, sliced
1 large can (6 to 7 ounces drained
    weight) pitted ripe olives, drained
    and sliced
1 red onion, diced
2 6-ounce jars marinated artichoke
    hearts
¼ cup minced fresh parsley
2 teaspoons minced garlic
¼ cup tarragon vinegar
1 tablespoon sugar
1½ teaspoons salt
¾ teaspoon Tabasco sauce

In a large nonreactive bowl, combine the green beans, kidney beans, celery, mushrooms, olives, and onion. Drain the artichoke hearts, reserving the oil. Cut each artichoke heart lengthwise into eighths and add to the vegetables along with the parsley.

In a jar, combine the reserved artichoke oil, garlic, vinegar, sugar, salt, and Tabasco sauce. Shake to mix well and pour over the vegetables. Toss well to coat.

Cover the bowl and refrigerate for several hours, to allow the flavors to develop.

Serve cold or at toom temperature.

Serves 8 to 10

⭒⭒⭒⭒⭒

BUTTERMILK PIE

A clear candidate for all-time best comfort food, Beverly Jacomini's buttermilk pie is puffed and golden when it comes out of the oven. As it cools, it falls to a sweet, soothing pie that's softer than homemade flan and equally good.

- 1 cup sugar
- 3 tablespoons all-purpose flour
- 2 large eggs, beaten
- 8 tablespoons (1 stick) unsalted butter, melted
- 1 cup buttermilk
- 2 teaspoon vanilla extract
- 1 9-inch unbaked pie shell, chilled (page 72)

Preheat the oven to 425°F.

In a bowl, thoroughly combine the sugar, flour, and eggs. Add the melted butter and buttermilk and stir until well mixed. Stir in the vanilla.

Pour the filling into the chilled pie shell and bake for 10 minutes.

Without opening the oven door, lower the oven temperature to 350°F. and bake for 35 minutes more. It is important to keep the oven door closed.

Transfer the pie to a wire rack to cool to room temperature. Cut into wedges to serve.

Serves 6 to 8

☆☆☆☆☆

Stainless steel shelves hold baskets and pottery used for kitchen tasks. Containers of homemade pickles, jellies, and jams are the result of a fertile country garden and Beverly's canning talents.

MENU

Fiesta Tamales

*New Mexican–Style
Spareribs*

Chile Verde

Garden Salad with Jícama

Flour Tortillas

Natillas

White Sangría

**The cuisine of northern New
Mexico, inspired by several native
cultures, requires hours of
preparation, but the result is
worth it. This banquet consists of
chile verde containing chunks of
pork, to be served in clay bowls
made by the cook, flour tortillas,
a salad with distinctive
New Mexican ingredients,
hand-rolled tamales, and
oven-baked spareribs.**

Galisteo, New Mexico

Twenty-five miles from Santa Fe, New Mexico, is the town of Galisteo, a walled Spanish colonial village where cottonwood trees practically outnumber people. Near this tiny enclave in the middle of a flat rocky desert is the traditional adobe hacienda of noted potter Priscilla Hoback and her husband, furniture designer Peter Gould. Their home is an oasis of friendship and hospitality, where icy sangría and such local specialties as Chile Verde or Fiesta Tamales make visits memorable.

Priscilla was raised on northern New Mexican home cooking by her mother, Rosalea Murphy, whose restaurant, The Pink Adobe, is a Santa Fe landmark. "Growing up with a mother who's a wonderful cook certainly is a bonus," says Priscilla. "I think I learned to cook by osmosis," and, it must be added, by her own highly skilled potter's hands. Priscilla would throw a ceramic platter or bowl in her studio and then go in search of the recipes to fill it from notable regional cooks, including Lucy del Gado, New Mexico's legendary food authority. "We would trade with each other,"

Priscilla recalls. "I'd give Lucy a plate or a pot and she would bring it back containing some delicious dish and the recipe for it. That's how I learned authentic southwestern cooking."

An evening built around the native cuisine, which draws on Spanish, Mexican, and Indian cultures and includes ingredients like piñon nuts, chile peppers, and blue maize, is the couple's favorite way to entertain. Guests sit at a long Texas Country table, handcrafted by Peter, in a dining room with tile floors, adobe walls, and handcarved ceiling beams, or vigas—elements that richly express the style of the Southwest.

"I do everything I can in advance," says Priscilla, not only because her studio schedule is so demanding but also because the meals she likes to serve are often complex and time-consuming to prepare. She makes tamales from scratch in the traditional manner and slow-cooks the meats and other fillings to build up layers of flavor.

"I put most of my energy into the main course," Priscilla notes, citing her New Mexican–style spareribs and an

unusual baked salmon entrée she once served on her husband's birthday. "I wrapped a whole salmon in lettuce leaves, covered it with cheesecloth, and packed it in wet clay from the studio. Then I baked it in my kitchen oven at a high heat until the clay cracked and the fish was done to perfection," a technique most appropriate for this potter who cooks.

Priscilla Hoback leads a horse from the corral on her property.

FIESTA TAMALES

"The secret to great tamales is to steam them and let them cool completely. Then I just resteam them before serving—they're delicious!" says Priscilla, who serves five or six varieties of tamales during the course of a year. This particular filling combination is an all-time favorite. If you own a pressure cooker, use it here. You'll save a great deal of time over steaming the usual way.

½ **pound dried cornhusks (available at specialty food shops)**

MASA

1 **16-ounce can white hominy**

¼ **cup vegetable oil**

½ **cup chopped green chiles**

¼ **teaspoon salt**

FILLING

1 **cup grated Cheddar cheese**

1 **cup grated Monterey Jack cheese**

½ **cup coarsely chopped green chiles**

¼ **cup whole piñon nuts**

¼ **cup minced onion**

1 **garlic clove, minced**

1 **teaspoon dried oregano**

½ **teaspoon salt**

Soak the cornhusks in hot water to cover until soft and pliable, about 2 hours, or cover with a large quantity of boiling water until soft, approximately 20 minutes.

Meanwhile, prepare the *masa:* Drain the hominy and reserve the liquid. Using a food processor fitted with a metal blade, combine the hominy, oil, chiles, and salt. Process until the mixture is thick and falls from a spoon like oatmeal. If the mixture is too thick, add 1 to 2 tablespoons of the reserved liquid and process again. Turn the masa into a bowl and set it aside.

In a bowl, combine all of the filling ingredients. Set aside.

Drain the cornhusks and divide them into groups by size. Pull off 12 to 18 long thin strips of husk that can be used to tie the tamales.

Thinly spread a generous teaspoon of the masa mixture over the center of one large husk or two smaller ones overlapped side by side. (There will be a large area of husk that is uncovered by masa.)

Mound an ample tablespoon of filling over the masa and fold in the side edges of the husk. Fold the top and bottom over to enclose the masa and filling and tie securely with a cornhusk strip, to create a small tied bundle. Take care that each tamale is tightly wrapped and closed. Continue stuffing the husks until all of the filling is used.

If using a pressure cooker, steam the tamales at 15 pounds of pressure for 1 hour. If using a conventional steamer, line the steamer basket and sides with a solid layer of cornhusks. Stand the tamales inside and top with another layer of cornhusks. Cover tightly and steam for 2 to 2½ hours, replenishing the water as necessary. Let the tamales cool completely, to let the flavors develop.

To serve, reheat the tamales in a steamer for approximately 10 to 20 minutes, just until heated through.

Makes 12 to 18 tamales

NEW MEXICAN–STYLE SPARERIBS

These ribs offer tender, flavorful meat that practically falls off the bone.

8 pounds pork spareribs

SAUCE

12 dried New Mexican chile pods, seeds
    removed and cut up or torn into
    pieces, or 1 cup *chile ancho* powder
    (available at specialty stores)

 1 cup ketchup

 2 tablespoons Worcestershire sauce

 2 tablespoons powdered mustard

 4 large garlic cloves

 2 tablespoons dried oregano

 2 tablespoons cumin seeds
    Freshly ground black pepper

Put the ribs in a large, deep nonreactive baking pan.

Make the sauce: Using a food processor fitted with a metal blade, combine all of the sauce ingredients and add 2 cups of water. Process until the chiles and garlic are puréed and the mixture is liquid. If the mixture seems too thick, add up to 1 cup more water.

Pour the sauce over the ribs and marinate at room temperature for at least 2 hours or cover and refrigerate overnight.

Preheat the oven to 350°F. Bake the ribs, basting, if desired, for 3 hours, or until they are very tender. Serve hot.

Serves 6 to 8

Just as Priscilla's cooking style is strongly influenced by her New Mexican environment, the pottery she makes in her studio (above) reflects the colors and textures of the Southwest. Two Indian-inspired examples sit on the windowsill with a carved folk art deer (right).

CHILE VERDE

Cooked beef or chicken could easily be substituted for the pork in this version.

20 to 25 poblano chiles (3 to 3½
    pounds), roasted and peeled
5 tablespoons (⅝ stick) unsalted butter
5 tablespoons vegetable oil
3 large garlic cloves, minced
1 large onion, chopped
¾ cup all-purpose flour
4 to 6 cups boiling chicken stock or
    broth
2 teaspoons ground cumin
1½ teaspoons dried oregano
    Salt
1 teaspoon freshly ground black pepper
2 to 2½ pounds thin-cut pork chops or
    pork shoulder, trimmed and cubed

Use your fingers to pull apart the chiles or coarsely chop them. Place the chiles in a large bowl and add cold water to cover. Set aside.

In a large heavy saucepan, melt the butter with 3 tablespoons of the oil over moderate heat. Add the garlic and onion and sauté until the onion is very soft, about 8 minutes.

Remove from the heat, add the flour, and stir until well combined. Return the pot to moderate heat and cook, stirring constantly, until the roux turns dark golden brown, 8 to 10 minutes.

Add 4 cups of the boiling stock and stir until incorporated into the roux. Drain the green chiles and add them along with the cumin, oregano, salt to taste, and pepper. Simmer for 35 minutes. If the chili is thicker than you like, add up to 2 cups more stock.

In a large skillet, warm the remaining 2 tablespoons of oil over moderate heat. Add the cubed pork and sauté until cooked through, about 5 minutes.

Divide the chunks of pork among individual soup bowls or stir them into the Chile Verde. Serve hot, accompanied by flour tortillas.

Serves 6 to 8

NATILLAS

A northern New Mexican tradition, this mousselike dessert is soothing after a spicy meal.

2½ cups whole milk, scalded
¾ cup sugar
3 tablespoons cornstarch
4 large eggs, separated and at room
    temperature
1 tablespoon vanilla extract, preferably
    Mexican vanilla
    Beaten sweetened whipped cream,
    ground cinnamon, and orange
    slices for serving

Put the milk into the top of a double boiler over simmering water. Add the sugar and cornstarch and whisk until the sugar has completely dissolved.

In a bowl, beat together the egg yolks. Slowly add the yolks to the milk, whisking to combine them. Cook gently, whisking all the while, until thickened enough to coat the back of a spoon, 15 to 18 minutes.

Remove from the heat and stir in the vanilla. Place a sheet of plastic wrap directly on the surface of the custard and let it cool to room temperature.

In a bowl, beat the egg whites until stiff and glossy. Fold the whites into the cooled custard. Spoon the mixture into stemmed glasses or dessert coupes and chill until set, about 1 hour.

To serve, smooth a thin layer of whipped cream over the custard and sprinkle it lightly with cinnamon. Garnish each glass with an orange slice.

Serves 8 to 10

A smooth finish to a spicy meal of local specialties, the natilla is a New Mexican version of mousse.

WHITE SANGRÍA

The ingredients for a good white sangría can vary, depending on what's handy and in season. Use a fruity dry white wine (it doesn't have to be expensive) and add chopped fruit to taste. Peaches, apples, pears, strawberries, raspberries, lemons, and limes will work well, but avoid highly acid fruit like fresh pineapple that won't go with the wine. Combine a large quantity of wine (about a gallon) with the fruit and add a quart or so of seltzer or club soda. A shot or two of fruit-flavored brandy can add special flavor as well.

An adobe church against a deep-blue sky is a typical New Mexican sight (above). The property includes twig fencing and weathered wood buildings for the help and horses (right). Casa de Hoback, outside of Galisteo, is an adobe with some Spanish Colonial detailing (left).

HOME FOR CHILLY WEATHER

New York,
New York

Lyn Hutchings (right) tailors her entertaining to the limited space available in her New York apartment. With husband, Doug Palermo, and baby, Olivia (above), she shops for fruit and vegetables at a local market.

There was a time when I would think nothing of inviting three hundred people to dinner and serving roast suckling pig," says Lyn Hutchings, another one of my very good friends. We met years ago when I worked for *Mademoiselle* and Lyn was just starting out in the interior design business. She is the greatest weekend guest because she makes herself at home in the kitchen and just starts cooking wonderful meals that look as easy to create as opening up a box of corn flakes!

I have always loved the way Lyn travels with her recipe book, a loose-leaf binder filled with her own personal favorites and ones she clips from magazines and newspapers. A former student of the famous cooking instructor Maurice Moore-Betty, who gave classes in his nineteenth-century carriage house on the Upper East Side in Manhattan, she can turn even a humble dish like meat loaf into a work of art in flavor, color, and texture.

Her meat loaf is an adaptation of her mother's recipe, which Lyn liked so much she'd "eat it cold for breakfast!" And I like it so much, I put in a special request for it whenever I get homesick for home cooking, usually after I've been on the road.

"From Maurice, I also learned to practice quality in everything I cooked," she says. "When we sat down to eat after a class, it was always at a table set with good linens and fine china and crystal." Her table settings invariably show this attention to detail.

The value of being organized was another lesson Lyn learned from the English-born cook. "The first thing we did in every class was analyze the menu and then map out a cooking strategy so that all the dishes would be ready at the same time and at the peak of their flavor," she explains. But it may well be that the small confines of Moore-Betty's antique kitchen taught Lyn her most valuable cooking lesson. "The limited space forced us to learn good habits. We cleaned as we went along," a habit she practices and preaches to this day. "The key to making a small kitchen work is assigning a 'home' to everything and cleaning and putting each tool or dish back in its home when you're finished with it."

Spur-of-the-moment dinner parties suit Lyn's life-style best these days, as her time is now divided between an interior design career and marriage to realtor Doug Palermo and their baby daughter, Olivia. "I try to keep a cache of ingredients in my freezer that I can call upon at the last minute," such as fresh herb butters to stuff under the

Even an old family standby like meat loaf shows flair when an accomplished cook follows her instincts for preparing and presenting food.

MENU

Mother's Meat Loaf

Green Beans Parmesan

Leafy Green Salad with Red Pepper Flake Vinaigrette

Apple Crisp

California or Washington State Merlot

Spatter-painted plates, French bistro glasses, and a collection of ceramic fruits and vegetables bring the host's personal style to the table (right). Apple crisp (far right) goes from the familiar to the sublime with the addition of Cognac, ginger, and cinnamon.

skin of chicken, pesto sauce (which she makes with walnuts and Parmesan), and her patented tomato sauce with pimientos, herbs, and sun-dried tomatoes.

Lyn's food preferences these days also reflect her enthusiasm for a more healthful life regimen. "I changed my eating habits about eight years ago and began to get away from heavy foods and starches." Fresh vegetables and salads sparked with a spicy red vinaigrette have replaced rice and potatoes as accompaniments, and desserts are more likely to be a beautiful mélange of exotic fruits like quince, mango, papaya, and kiwi than a dense chocolate concoction. However, Lyn does admit to partaking of "fast foods" from time to time. "Some of our very best get-togethers have featured Japanese or Chinese dishes from a take-out place."

▼▼▼▼▼▼▼▼▼▼

MOTHER'S MEAT LOAF

Everyone who moves to the city brings along bits of home. Lyn Hutchings brought her mother's meat loaf, which she adapted to make her own.

MEAT LOAF

1½ **pounds ground top or bottom round beef**

½ **pound ground lean veal**

1 **medium sweet green pepper, finely diced**

1 **medium sweet red pepper, finely diced, or ½ to ¾ cup chopped pimientos**

1 **small onion, finely diced**

½ **cup finely diced celery**

1 **garlic clove, minced**

2 **tablespoons chili sauce**

¼ **cup ketchup**

¼ **cup freshly grated Parmesan cheese**

½ **large egg, lightly beaten**

1½ **tablespoons fresh thyme leaves, whole or chopped, or ¾ teaspoon dried thyme**

2 **teaspoons dried oregano**

1 **tablespoon coarse (kosher) salt, or to taste**

1 **teaspoon freshly ground black pepper Pinch of cayenne pepper**

1 **tablespoon Worcestershire sauce, or to taste Tabasco sauce to taste**

2 **bacon slices (optional)**

4 **bay leaves (optional)**

SAUCE

⅓ **cup chili sauce**

⅓ **cup ketchup**

Preheat the oven to 350°F. Line a 12-inch round baking pan with aluminum foil.

In a large bowl, combine the ground round, veal, sweet green and red peppers, onion, celery, garlic, Parmesan cheese, and egg. Sprinkle on the thyme, oregano, salt, black pepper, cayenne pepper, and Worcestershire and Tabasco sauces. Mix well to distribute the ingredients evenly.

Shape the meat mixture into a round loaf and set in the baking pan. Crisscross the bacon slices over the top of the meat loaf and tuck the end of a bay leaf under each strip, if desired.

In a measuring cup, combine the chili sauce and ketchup. Brush a generous coating of the sauce over the top of the meat loaf. (The meat loaf can be made ahead to this point and refrigerated. Let it come to room temperature before baking.)

Bake the meat loaf, basting frequently with the remaining sauce, for 45 minutes. Turn off the oven and leave the loaf in the oven for 15 minutes more. Do not overcook.

Transfer the meat loaf to a platter and cut it into thin slices at the table.

Serves 6

GREEN BEANS PARMESAN

Fresh green beans are a colorful accompaniment to meat loaf.

- 2 pounds long green beans, trimmed
- 1 teaspoon baking soda
- 6 tablespoons (¾ stick) unsalted butter
- ¼ to ½ cup freshly grated Parmesan cheese

Bring a large pot of water to a boil over high heat. Add the beans and baking soda and cook for 3 to 4 minutes, or until the beans are crisp-tender and bright green.

Meanwhile, in a small saucepan, melt the butter over moderately low heat. Remove the pan from the heat and stir in the Parmesan cheese.

Drain the beans and turn them into a warm serving bowl. Pour the butter sauce over the beans and toss to coat thoroughly. Serve hot.

Serves 6

LEAFY GREEN SALAD WITH RED PEPPER FLAKE VINAIGRETTE

SALAD

- 2 medium heads green leafy lettuce, such as Boston or lamb's lettuce
- 1 small head radicchio or red-leaf lettuce
- 1 medium Belgian endive

VINAIGRETTE

- 2 tablespoons red or white wine vinegar
- 3 tablespoons olive oil
- 1 teaspoon Dijon mustard
- 1 teaspoon coarse (kosher) salt
  Freshly ground black pepper
  Crushed red pepper flakes

Wash and dry the greens. Arrange them in a bowl. Tuck in the radicchio on one side of the bowl. Separate the endive leaves and arrange on the other side. Combine the vinaigrette ingredients in a jar with a tight-fitting lid and shake well. Just before serving, pour the vinaigrette over the greens or pass it separately at the table.

Serves 6

APPLE CRISP

- ⅔ cup dark raisins
- ¼ cup Cognac or brandy
- 6 apples, such as 3 Granny Smiths and 3 McIntoshes or Cortlands
- 3 tablespoons fresh lemon juice
- ¾ cup uncooked oatmeal (not instant)
- ¾ cup firmly packed dark brown sugar
- ½ cup all-purpose flour
- 1½ teaspoons ground cinnamon

- ½ teaspoon ground ginger
- ¼ teaspoon ground nutmeg
- ¼ teaspoon salt
- 8 tablespoons (1 stick) butter, softened

FLAVORED WHIPPED CREAM TOPPING

- 1 cup whipping cream
- ¼ teaspoon ground ginger
- ¼ teaspoon ground cinnamon

In a small bowl, combine the raisins and Cognac and set aside for several hours or overnight.

Preheat the oven to 350°F. Butter a large ovenproof bowl. Peel, core, and thinly slice the apples. Place them in a bowl and toss with the lemon juice.

In another bowl, combine the oatmeal, sugar, flour, cinnamon, ginger, nutmeg, and salt. Add the butter and stir until crumbly and well mixed.

Drain the raisins and combine with the apples. Turn the fruit into the prepared bowl and sprinkle on the topping to cover completely. Bake for 35 to 40 minutes, or until browned.

Make the topping: In a bowl, beat the cream until lightly whipped. Add the ginger and cinnamon and beat to desired consistency. Cover and refrigerate.

Serve the crisp warm or at room temperature with the whipped topping.

Serves 4 to 6

Southampton, Long Island

The chicken curry buffet (right) is served from an 18th-century French wine-tasting table with a traditional American centerpiece of the fall bounty. Mary and Ed Higgins are shown with children Bartley and Margot and friend Dara Mandle in the dining room of their Federal-style weekend home (above).

A beloved Irish grandmother who cooked for clan-size family gatherings is the inspiration behind the entertaining style of Mary Higgins. Mary and I have been neighbors and dear friends for years and I love hearing her reminisce about her Philadelphia childhood and the woman who influenced her so strongly.

"Grandma was a wonderful cook and thought nothing of making supper for ten every night and for as many as thirty-five on Sundays, when all the relatives would gather at our house," Mary recalls. "Her love for her family was in her cooking. At mealtime, she would always wait until everyone had sat down before taking her place. Then she'd await our verdict. She would be so pleased when we'd tell her how much we liked what she had prepared. Her pride was on the table and she deeply appreciated receiving her just due."

Grandmother's legacy is evident in the competent and confident way Mary goes about hosting her own curry chicken dinner every fall in her Southampton, Long Island, home. Mary, attorney husband Ed, and their three children live in this handsome Federal-style house, circa 1830, full time during the summer and on weekends the rest of the year. The buffet is so popular with friends—we've insisted that Mary make it an October tradition—because

it's a chance to savor good home cooking in a relaxed setting and informal atmosphere.

The buffet is laid out on a French wine-taster's table from the eighteenth century that's dressed up with decorations in suitably autumnal colors. The Higginses' friends, usually about thirty in number, flow through the house warmed by four fireplaces and the geniality of the host and hostess.

"Our attitude when we give a party is that we want to have as good a time as our guests," says Mary. "There's no point in going to the trouble of all the preparations and then feeling overwhelmed by the company."

Mary avoids time pressures by planning and preparing her dinner early. "I purposely choose recipes that can be made in advance," she says. "I shop two or three days ahead of time, set the table a day early, and get the meal itself ready by noon of the day of the party."

Long ago, Mary learned the value of building some margin for error into her entertaining plans. "I had invited sixty guests to help us celebrate our first wedding anniversary," she recalls. "The day before, I brought home one hundred and eighty chicken cutlets from the butcher, cooked them up in a huge vat of curry, and put them in the refrigerator to cool overnight. But the fridge wasn't working properly and the

MENU

Chicken Curry

Curry Condiments

White Rice

Bibb, Watercress, and Endive Salad with Shallot Vinaigrette

French Bread

Lemon Mousse

Assorted Cookies

Squash, gourds, and pumpkins from a roadside stand bring autumn's colors into the house.

cutlets continued to cook until they were the consistency of erasers. Luckily, I had time to start all over again the next morning!"

Thanks to her Irish grandmother and an Irish sense of humor, Mary handles the task of entertaining as if it were no task at all.

~~~~~~

CHICKEN CURRY

Curry is the most adaptable dish—a cook can add or detract from the seasonings to suit the guests or occasion. If you have fresh flaked or grated coconut, do not hesitate to add it to this fruity curry.

12 tablespoons (1½ sticks) unsalted butter
2 large onions, chopped
3 celery stalks, diced
3 large garlic cloves, minced
¼ cup chopped fresh parsley
2 bay leaves
1 1-inch piece fresh ginger, peeled and minced
3 tart apples, such as Granny Smiths, peeled and diced
2 ripe pears, peeled and diced
1 teaspoon powdered mustard
½ teaspoon crushed red pepper flakes
¾ pound baked Virginia ham, diced
5 tablespoons all-purpose flour
2 teaspoons ground mace
 About ¼ cup curry powder, or more to taste
3 tablespoons *garam masala* (optional)
1 teaspoon salt
5 cups chicken stock or broth
3 large boneless, skinless chicken breasts (about 3 pounds total weight), trimmed and cut into 1-inch cubes
6 tablespoons cream of coconut
¾ cup golden raisins

In a large stockpot or Dutch oven, melt the butter over moderate heat. When the foam subsides, add the onions, celery, garlic, parsley, bay leaves, ginger, apples, pears, mustard, and crushed pepper flakes. Cook, stirring occasionally, for 10 minutes, or until the vegetables are very soft.

Stir in the ham until it is coated with butter. Stir in the flour, mace, curry powder, *garam masala* (if you are using it), and salt. Turn the heat to moderately low and cook, stirring from time to time, for 5 minutes.

Add the chicken stock and bring almost to a boil over moderately high heat. Turn the heat to low, cover, and simmer for 1 hour.

Using a slotted spoon, remove about

Small pumpkins, hollowed out and lined with foil, make unusual but eminently practical vessels for curry condiments.

half of the solids. Place the solids in a fine sieve and rub the vegetables through the sieve with the back of a wooden spoon to purée them. Return the purée to the pot.

Add the cubed chicken and simmer until tender, 8 to 10 minutes.

Stir in the coconut cream and raisins. Serve at once with white rice or let cool, cover, and refrigerate for up to 2 days; the flavor will improve with time. Let the curry come to room temperature before reheating and serving it.

Serves 8 to 10

CURRY CONDIMENTS

Since Mary Higgins serves this meal every autumn, she tries to incorporate a seasonal look in the buffet. Small orange pumpkins make excellent

serving bowls for these condiments. Shallow bowls or custard cups can be fit inside the pumpkins to hold wet mixtures, such as chutneys.

8 to 12 small pumpkins (about 6 to 8 inches in diameter)

2 to 3 sweet red peppers, diced

2 to 3 sweet green peppers, diced

2 to 3 bunches scallions (including the green parts), sliced

1 to 2 large red onions, chopped

2 to 3 firm ripe tomatoes, peeled, seeded, and diced

½ to ¾ pound peanuts (whole or pieces)

½ to ¾ pound cashews (whole or pieces)

2 cups golden raisins

1 8½-ounce jar Major Grey's Chutney

1 cup homemade or store-bought apple chutney

1 cup homemade or store-bought peach chutney

Using a sharp chef's knife, cut off and discard the top of each pumpkin at the shoulder so the shape resembles a deep bowl. Remove and discard the strings and seeds or reserve the seeds, toast them in a moderate oven, and serve as an additional condiment. Drain the pumpkins upside down for up to 2 days.

Pat the insides of the pumpkins dry with paper towels. Line the cavities with aluminum foil or plastic wrap, if desired; this is particularly necessary with moist condiments and other foods that should not become soggy, such as peanuts and cashews.

Prepare the vegetables and keep chilled in bags in the refrigerator. Fill the pumpkin bowls just before serving.

BIBB, WATERCRESS, AND ENDIVE SALAD WITH SHALLOT VINAIGRETTE

2 heads Bibb or Boston lettuce

2 to 3 bunches watercress

4 to 5 heads endive

SHALLOT VINAIGRETTE

¼ cup white wine vinegar

3 tablespoons minced shallots

1 large egg yolk, at room temperature

1 tablespoon Dijon mustard

1 teaspoon Worcestershire sauce

Salt and freshly ground black pepper

1 cup olive oil

Wash and dry the greens. Tear them into bite-size pieces and refrigerate in plastic bags.

Using a food processor, blender, or jar with a tight-fitting lid, combine the vinegar, shallots, egg yolk, mustard, Worcestershire sauce, and salt and pepper to taste. Blend until well combined. Slowly drizzle in the oil and mix well until incorporated.

Just before serving, put the greens in a salad bowl and pour the vinaigrette over them. Toss lightly to coat.

Serves 8 to 10

Endive leaves are the star attractions in the salad, a cooling accompaniment to spicy Indian fare.

LEMON MOUSSE

This is a refreshing, palate-cleansing after-dinner sweet. It can be made days ahead of the party.

- 1 envelope unflavored gelatin
- 10 large eggs, separated and at room temperature
- 1½ cups sugar
- ¾ cup fresh lemon juice
- 2 tablespoons finely grated lemon rind
- 1 cup whipping cream

In a small bowl, dissolve the gelatin in 3 tablespoons of cold water and set aside.

In a medium bowl, beat the egg yolks with an electric mixer until frothy and lemon-colored. Gradually add the sugar, beating thoroughly until dissolved.

Add the lemon juice and lemon rind and mix thoroughly.

Turn the yolk mixture into the top of a double boiler and cook, stirring constantly, over simmering water until the mixture thickens and easily coats the back of a spoon, 10 to 12 minutes.

Remove the mixture from the heat and stir in the dissolved gelatin. Set aside to cool to room temperature, or place the pan in a bowl of ice water and stir until the mixture cools to room temperature.

Meanwhile, in a medium bowl, beat the egg whites until they form soft peaks. One-third at a time, gently fold the whites into the cooled yolk mixture until no white streaks remain. Cover and refrigerate.

In a chilled bowl, beat the cream until soft peaks form. One-third at a time, fold the cream into the mousse until the mixture is an even color.

Pour the mousse into dessert coupes, stemmed glasses, or a soufflé dish and refrigerate until set, 3 to 4 hours.

Serves 8 to 10

Lemon mousse is offered in a yellow spongeware bowl with silver concho pattern dessert spoon (above). Spare elements, including an old harvest basket, make an effective seasonal display over the mantel (below left).

A TRIP TO PENNSYLVANIA

West Chester, Pennsylvania

PENNSYLVANIA DUTCH COUNTRY COOKING AT AUDREY AND DOUG JULIAN'S

Modern conveniences are concealed behind a counter built of wide wood planks in this Colonial kitchen (below), where Audrey Julian applies finishing touches to her menu.

Warming a table set with hearty cold weather fare (right), the hearth is adorned with implements used by early American cooks. Blue sponge design on redware plates is the signature of a local potter.

Situated at a historic five-point intersection in West Chester, where the Battle of Brandywine was fought in 1777, the Dillingworthtown Country Store is the home of Audrey and Doug Julian. The stuccoed stone building has been in continuous use as a store since 1758. The Julians have retained the original landlord's name for the establishment, but have replaced the general store inventory with antique and reproduction Country primitive furnishings and folk art. Save for the kitchen and bathrooms, the family quarters still appear as they might have in Colonial times.

"I loved old things long before they were ever popular," says Audrey. "We lived with Danish modern when we were first married, thirty-five years ago. That lasted about three years—until I brought home my first dry sink."

A seasonal cook who takes her cue from a plentiful herb garden—she grows some fifty varieties in four separate planting areas—Audrey is accomplished at Country fare, much of it influenced by the local Pennsylvania Dutch community. Her German-style roast pork dinner, a family favorite, comes complete with heart-shaped corn muffins. The rustic table is set with redware plates made by an area craftsman, Beaumont salt glaze pottery, and homespun linens. It is a warming, stick-to-your-ribs meal that is ideal when the days get cooler. With it she serves apple butter, corn relish, cottage cheese, and piccalilli relish as adaptations of sweet-and-sour condiments.

The unique historic home is the inspiration for a lot of Audrey's entertaining. When she hosts her annual "tavern party" for friends and family in the fall, the house is lit entirely by candlelight and the children dress up in Colonial costumes. At Christmas, the rooms are festooned with ropes of evergreen and holly and the hearths have big kettles of wassail simmering.

"When you look out the windows at the rolling hills, split rail fences, and eighteenth-century buildings, it's hard to believe that a major interstate highway runs by only a few miles away," says Audrey, standing in the keeping room of her prerevolutionary house.

MENU

Roast Pork with Sauerkraut

Fried Apples and Bacon

Heart-Shaped
Corn Muffins

Cherry Cobbler

A roast pork and sauerkraut recipe from the Pennsylvania Dutch provides a plateful of rich fall flavors.

ROAST PORK WITH SAUERKRAUT

The roast turns out to be wonderfully tender and juicy—and the sauerkraut is so tasty that even those who don't like it would love it sweetened this way with the juices from the roast pork. Buy fresh sauerkraut, if you can find it, or the kind that's packaged in plastic bags; it's much crisper and tastier than the canned type.

1 4½- to 5-pound boneless pork roast (Ask your butcher to leave some of the fat on the top of the roast.)
Salt and freshly ground black pepper
2 2-pound packages sauerkraut, rinsed and drained
4 tart green apples, such as Granny Smiths, peeled, cored, and cut into thick slices
1 medium onion, diced
½ to ¾ cup firmly packed light brown sugar (depending on the sweetness of the apples)
2 teaspoons prepared mustard
1 teaspoon caraway seeds
¾ cup dry white wine

Preheat the oven to 450°F.

Rub the pork roast with salt and pepper. Put it in a large roasting pan and put in the oven, turning it to brown on all sides, 20 to 30 minutes. Remove the roast and lower the oven temperature to 250°F.

Scatter the sauerkraut all around the roast. In a bowl, mix together the apples, onion, sugar, mustard, and caraway seeds. Sprinkle this mixture over the sauerkraut and drizzle the wine over all. Cover and roast at 250°F. for about 4 hours, or until the meat is well done yet very tender. Do not let the roast dry out. (If there was not too much fat on the roast, you might want to moisten it with additional wine.)

Let the roast rest for about 10 minutes before slicing and serving it.

Serves 4 to 6

FRIED APPLES AND BACON

The sweet and salty combination of apples and bacon sets off the rich flavor of the pork roast. I wouldn't serve one without the other.

½ pound sliced bacon
3 to 4 large tart apples, such as Winesaps

Without separating the slices, cut the bacon crosswise into four equal sections. Render the bacon in a large skillet over moderate heat until the slices separate and the bacon is crisp. Remove the bacon and drain on paper towels.

Meanwhile, core and slice the apples; you may peel them if desired. Pour off all but ¼ cup of the bacon fat and place the skillet over moderate heat. Add the apples and cook, stirring, until they are tender but not mushy. Add the bacon and toss. Serve hot with the pork roast.

Serves 4 to 6

As down home as the cast-iron skillet in which it is served is this salty sweet concoction of fried apples and bacon (above). Under a panoply of old and reproduction baskets, the tavern table in the keeping room (below) is laid out with salt-glaze pottery and blue-and-white homespun linens.

CHERRY COBBLER

8 tablespoons (1 stick) unsalted butter,
   softened
1 cup sugar
1 large egg
1 cup all-purpose flour
½ teaspoon baking powder
1 17-ounce can pitted tart cherries,
   drained

Preheat the oven to 375°F. Butter a
10-inch pie plate or other baking dish.

In a bowl, beat the butter with the
sugar until fluffy. Add the egg and beat
until light. Add the flour and baking
powder and beat until well combined.

Place the cherries in the prepared
baking dish and spoon the batter over
them. Do not try to cover the cherries
completely; the batter will rise and
spread out, and, besides, it's good if the
fruit bubbles through.

Bake for 40 to 50 minutes, or until
the top is browned and the fruit is bubbly. Serve warm with whipped cream or
ice cream.

Serves 4 to 6

HEART-SHAPED
CORN MUFFINS

1 cup yellow cornmeal
1 cup all-purpose flour
¼ cup sugar (optional)
1 tablespoon plus 1 teaspoon baking
   powder
½ teaspoon salt
1 cup milk
1 large egg
¼ cup vegetable shortening

*A folk art whaler boy (top) seems to
cast a hungry eye in the
direction of the heart-shaped corn
muffins. Even the after-dinner
divertissement is in the spirit of
prerevolutionary times. While the
cherry cobbler (above) disappears,
checkers will advance on an old
painted breadboard (right).*

Preheat the oven to 425°F. Generously grease heart-shaped or regular
muffin tins or corn-stick molds.

In a bowl, stir together the cornmeal,
flour, sugar, baking powder, and salt.
Add the milk, egg, and shortening and
beat until fairly smooth, approximately
1 minute.

Divide the batter among the prepared cups or molds and bake for 15 to
20 minutes, or until golden brown.

Makes about 1½ dozen

The stone and stucco building (top), in continuous operation as a country store since 1758, now serves as both home and shop for the Julian family. Folk artist Nancy Thomas with husband, Charles (above), brings a birdhouse she's made to be sold at the store.

159

Pike Place Market in downtown Seattle is the oldest farm and fish market in America. It clings to its traditions of personal service and a selection of foods from around the world.

WILD RICE AND BROWN RICE WITH MUSHROOMS

Like the salmon, this recipe reflects the popularity of mushrooms in the Northwest.

> 1 cup wild rice
>
> 1 cup brown rice
>
> 1 teaspoon salt
>
> 4 tablespoons (½ stick) unsalted butter
>
> 8 shallots, minced
>
> 2 cups sliced fresh mushrooms
>
> 1 small onion, minced
>
> 1 tablespoon chopped fresh oregano, or
>> ½ teaspoon dried oregano
>
> Chicken broth
>
> Salt and freshly ground black pepper

In a heavy saucepan, combine the wild rice with 3 cups of water and bring to a boil over high heat. Turn the heat to very low, cover tightly, and simmer for 1 hour. Drain well.

Meanwhile, in a heavy saucepan, combine the brown rice with 2 cups of water and the salt; bring to a boil over high heat. Turn the heat to very low, cover, and simmer for 45 minutes, or until all of the water has been absorbed.

Combine the two rices in a bowl and toss to mix well and separate the grains. Cover with aluminum foil and keep warm.

In a skillet, melt the butter over moderate heat and then add the shallots, mushrooms, onions, and oregano. Sauté until the vegetables are softened, about 5 minutes.

Scrape the vegetable mixture into the rice and toss. Add just enough chicken broth to moisten and season with salt and pepper to taste. Recover with the foil and check the seasonings before serving.

Serves 8 to 10

CRUNCHY OAT AND CRANBERRY MUFFINS

These fiber-filled muffins are as tasty as they are nutritious.

- ¾ cup all-purpose flour
- ¾ cup whole wheat flour
- 1 cup uncooked oatmeal (not instant)
- ½ cup firmly packed light brown sugar
- 1 tablespoon baking powder
- 1 teaspoon salt
- 1 teaspoon ground cinnamon
- 1 cup cranberries (if frozen, thaw and drain)
- 4 tablespoons (½ stick) unsalted butter, melted
- 1 cup milk
- 1 large egg

Preheat the oven to 425°F. Lightly butter a 12-cup regular or heart-shaped muffin tin. In a bowl, combine the flours, oatmeal, sugar, baking powder, salt, and cinnamon.

Toss the cranberries with a table-spoon or two of the dry ingredients.

Beat together the butter, milk, and egg. Pour the mixture into the dry ingredients and mix. Add the cranberries and stir until well distributed.

Divide the batter among the muffin cups and bake for about 15 minutes, or until lightly browned. Let the muffins stand in the tins for about 5 minutes before unmolding.

Makes 1 dozen

WASHINGTON STATE APPLE CAKE

This fragrant apple cake is served at the Captain Whidbey Inn on Whidbey Island, about ninety miles north of Seattle. It makes the perfect ending to a seafood meal.

CAKE

- 3 large eggs
- 2 cups granulated sugar
- 1 cup vegetable oil

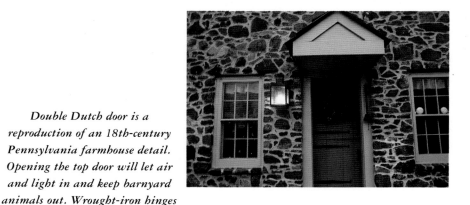

Double Dutch door is a reproduction of an 18th-century Pennsylvania farmhouse detail. Opening the top door will let air and light in and keep barnyard animals out. Wrought-iron hinges were hand-forged by a contemporary Seattle blacksmith.

- 2 cups all-purpose flour
- 1 teaspoon baking soda
- 2 teaspoons ground cinnamon
- 1 teaspoon vanilla extract
- 1 cup chopped walnuts
- 4 cups thinly sliced tart apples, preferably from Washington State

CREAM CHEESE ICING

- ¾ cup cream cheese, softened
- 4 tablespoons (½ stick) unsalted butter, softened
- 2 cups confectioners' sugar
- 1 teaspoon fresh lemon juice

Make the cake: Preheat the oven to 350°F. Generously butter a heart-shaped cake pan or a 9 x 13 x 2-inch baking dish.

In a large bowl, beat the eggs with an electric mixer until frothy. Add the sugar and the oil and beat until the sugar has dissolved. Combine all of the dry ingredients and add to the egg mixture along with the vanilla and walnuts.

Spread the apples over the bottom of the prepared baking pan and pour the batter over them. Smooth the top to completely cover the apples and bake for 1 hour. Set aside to cool to room temperature.

Make the icing: When the cake is cool, beat the cream cheese with the butter until fluffy. Gradually beat in the confectioners' sugar and lemon juice until well blended and creamy.

Unmold the cake and spread the icing over the top but not the sides.

Serves 8 to 10

Valentine to Washington State's apple crop is an old-fashioned apple cake baked in a heart-shaped mold. Glassware the color of cranberries was hand blown by a Colonial craftsman.

KANSAS FOR CHRISTMAS

Kansas City, Kansas

Until I've baked at least five different kinds of cookies, my husband, John, doesn't believe that Christmas has come," says Kathy Killip. "I have recipes handed down from my mother and my grandmother, and from friends." Kathy's cookies, like the natural wreaths and heart-shaped ornaments she creates for her studio, Underbrush Ltd., bear the stamp of an exceptional cook who is also an artist. "Some are Old World standards like *springerle, pfeffernuss,* and *keplings;* others I make in the shape of stars, doves, and the animals of the manger—which children especially enjoy—and dough cookies, which are my favorites, are made from my collection of antique molds."

Christmas Eve is when the Killip family—Kathy, John, and their three children, Whitney, Wyeth, and Brielle —sit down to a special dinner. Sharing tasks in and out of the kitchen (John does all the table appointments and flower arranging, while Kathy busies herself with preparations), the couple has always made the holiday an important part of family life. As newlyweds, the Killips thought nothing of inviting as many people as they could fit into a small apartment for what became their annual "Christmas in July" party. "I'd bake hundreds of cookies, we'd set up the tree, and each guest brought an ornament," remembers Kathy. "Over the years, the ornaments have provided us with special memories."

Traditionalists when it comes to Christmas dinner, Kathy and John like to serve goose with mushrooms they have gathered during summer outings in Colorado. "For thirty-six years, our family has spent summer vacations in the mountains near the small mining town of Crede. Here we forage for wild chanterelles, a tradition begun by my mother, who has made the study of edible wilds her hobby. Next to gathering them, eating them is the most exhilarating part," says Kathy. When they are brought out from the freezer for the holiday table, the taste of summer is still there.

Kathy and John draw on a cookbook collection of more than four hundred titles for inspiration in planning their entertaining menus. Not surprisingly in this artistic household, the food is presented as artfully as it is planned and prepared. "Attention to texture and color as well as taste makes preparing the food like designing a new piece of art," Kathy explains. "It's the difference between dumping green beans into a bowl and serving them in pretty bundles topped by pimientos cut into tiny heart shapes."

MENU

Cream of
Wild Mushroom Soup

Roast Goose

Wild Rice Casserole

Tomatoes Stuffed with
Mushrooms and Roquefort
Cheese

Bundled Green Beans Tied
with Chives

Cranberry Sauce

Swedish Kepling Cookies

Delicious Cutout
Sugar Cookies

Toffee Bars

The Christmas goose (above),
dressed in fresh sage leaves and
surrounded by red hearts and
cranberries, brings the
traditional aromas and colors
of the season to the house.
Feeding the ducks in the pond
near the house (left) is a Killip
family affair.

CREAM OF WILD MUSHROOM SOUP

Kathy's mother loves to go wild mushroom hunting. She created this recipe in 1981, when she gathered and froze over two hundred bags of wild mushrooms.

6 tablespoons (¾ stick) unsalted butter

1½ pounds wild mushrooms, such as King Boletus, Meadow, or chanterelles

1 medium onion, thinly sliced

½ cup all-purpose flour

3 14-ounce cans undiluted chicken broth, or 5¼ cups homemade chicken stock

1 tablespoon fresh lemon juice

¼ cup minced fresh parsley

3 cups half-and-half

Salt and freshly ground black pepper

½ cup dry vermouth

In a large heavy saucepan, melt the butter over moderate heat. Add the mushrooms and onion and sauté until the vegetables are limp but not browned and all of the moisture has evaporated. Set aside to cool for a few minutes.

Using a food processor fitted with a metal blade, finely chop the mushrooms and onion.

Return the mixture to the saucepan and place over moderate heat. Add the flour and cook, stirring, until well blended. Gradually add the broth, whisking constantly to prevent lumps from forming. Simmer the soup over low heat for 20 minutes.

Add the lemon juice and parsley and simmer for 5 minutes more. Stir in the half-and-half and simmer but do not

boil. Season with salt and pepper to taste and stir in the vermouth. Serve hot, in warmed soup bowls.

Serves 8

ROAST GOOSE

Buy the largest goose you can find and cook it long and slowly to melt the fat. Apples and onions will add plenty of flavor to the meat.

1 12- to 14-pound goose
  Salt
2 apples, quartered
2 onions, quartered

Preheat the oven to 325°F.

Wash and dry the goose, inside and out. Sprinkle salt in the cavity and place the apples and onions inside. Prick the skin all over with a sharp needle, taking care not to puncture the meat.

Place the goose in a roasting pan and roast, uncovered, for about 4 hours, or until dark golden brown and tender. Spoon off the fat from time time.

Put the goose on a decorative platter and garnish with bouquets of fresh herbs and flowers.

Serves 8

WILD RICE CASSEROLE

This is a rich, creamy combination of wild rice and mushrooms. If you're like Kathy and have a supply of wild mushrooms, by all means use them.

1 cup wild rice
10 tablespoons (1¼ sticks) unsalted butter

2 cups coarsely chopped wild or
    cultivated fresh mushrooms
¼ cup plus 1 tablespoon grated onion
3 tablespoons all-purpose flour
3 cups half-and-half
1 cup milk
  Salt and freshly ground black pepper
1¼ cups cracker crumbs
  Paprika (optional)

In a heavy saucepan, bring the wild rice and 4 cups of water to a boil over high heat. Turn the heat to very low and cook, tightly covered, for 1 hour. Drain the wild rice in a colander.

Preheat the oven to 350°F.

In a large skillet or saucepan, melt 6 tablespoons of the butter over moderate heat. Add the mushrooms and onion, and cook, stirring, until the moisture has evaporated.

Add the flour and cook, stirring, to make a roux. Gradually add the half-and-half and milk and cook, stirring constantly, until smooth and thick. Sea-

Chanterelles (far left), gathered in the mountains of Colorado on family vacations, sweeten the stock of a mushroom soup flavored with vermouth and parsley. A tree shimmering with hearts and hand-cast angels (left) is outshone by the enthusiasm of the children taking part in the ritual of Christmas morning. Cookie heart (below) sweetly seals a gift.

son with salt and pepper to taste.

Add the wild rice to the sauce and stir to mix well. Turn the mixture into a flat baking dish and set aside.

Melt the remaining 4 tablespoons of butter in a large skillet and stir in the crumbs. Cook, stirring constantly over moderate heat, until the crumbs are lightly browned.

Sprinkle the top of the wild rice mixture with the crumbs and stencil a paprika heart on top, if desired. Bake for 30 minutes and serve hot.

Serves 8

Encircled by an herbal wreath of parsley, sage, and thyme are baked tomato cups stuffed with fresh mushrooms and Roquefort cheese (above). Pimiento hearts garnish green bean bundles tied with chives (left). Antique rocking horse rides shotgun for a white-on-white display of children's dresses (right).

TOMATOES STUFFED WITH MUSHROOMS AND ROQUEFORT CHEESE

8 medium-to-large firm ripe tomatoes

8 tablespoons (1 stick) unsalted butter

1¼ pounds fresh mushrooms, sliced

1 cup sour cream

1 tablespoon plus 1 teaspoon all-purpose flour

3 ounces Roquefort cheese, at room temperature

¼ teaspoon *fines herbes*

¼ teaspoon dried sweet basil

¼ teaspoon lemon pepper

1 teaspoon chopped fresh parsley

2 tablespoons dry sherry

Salt and freshly ground black pepper

Sesame seeds

Paprika

Cut off the top of each tomato and scoop out the pulp and seeds, leaving a shell. Invert the tomato cups on paper towels to drain.

In a large skillet, melt the butter over moderate heat and sauté the mushrooms, stirring, until all of the moisture has evaporated.

In a bowl, stir together the sour cream and flour. Add the mixture to the mushrooms and stir over low heat to blend well. Stir in the Roquefort and cook until smooth. Add the *fines herbes*, basil, lemon pepper, parsley, sherry, and salt and pepper to taste and stir until well mixed. Set aside to cool.

Preheat the oven to 375°F.

Loosely stuff the tomatoes, dividing the mixture evenly among them. Place the stuffed tomatoes on a baking sheet and sprinkle with the sesame seeds and paprika. Bake for 15 minutes, or until bubbly, and serve hot.

Serves 8

CRANBERRY SAUCE

This is an orange-spiked variation of a holiday standard.

1¾ cups sugar

¾ cup fresh orange juice

4 cups fresh cranberries, washed and picked over

1½ tablespoons finely grated orange rind

In a heavy nonreactive saucepan, combine the sugar, orange juice, and ½ cup of water over low heat. Bring to a boil, washing down the sides of the pan with a brush dipped in cold water so that no sugar crystals remain. Cook the syrup for 5 minutes, or until the sugar has completely dissolved.

Add the cranberries and cook over moderately high heat for 4 to 5 minutes, or until the berries pop.

Remove from the heat, stir in the orange rind, and set aside to cool to room temperature. Scrape the sauce into a bowl or jar, cover, and chill well.

Makes about 1 quart

SWEDISH KEPLING COOKIES

These cookies are from one of Kathy's mother's recipes. With the toffee bars, they are John Killip's favorites.

½ pound (2 sticks) unsalted butter, softened

¼ cup confectioners' sugar plus sugar for dusting

1 teaspoon vanilla extract

Pinch of salt

½ cup ground pecans

2 cups all-purpose flour

Preheat the oven to 350°F.

Using a food processor, cream the butter until fluffy. Add the confectioners' sugar, vanilla, and salt and process until well combined. Scrape the mixture into a bowl and stir in the nuts.

Shape two large tablespoons of dough into small crescents, each about the diameter of your thumb and 2 to 3 inches in length. Place on baking sheets and bake for about 20 minutes, or until just lightly browned; do not let them get too brown.

Place additional confectioners' sugar on a shallow plate, and while the cookies are still hot, roll them in the sugar. Let cool before storing in airtight tins.

Makes 3 to 4 dozen

DELICIOUS CUTOUT SUGAR COOKIES

These simple cookies are Grandmother Didde's recipe—and are ideal for making fanciful shapes.

3 cups all-purpose flour
2 teaspoons baking powder
1 scant teaspoon baking soda
½ teaspoon ground nutmeg
½ pound (2 sticks) unsalted butter
2 large eggs
1 cup sugar
¼ cup milk
1 teaspoon vanilla extract
Colored sugar or cookie decorations
(optional)

In a bowl, combine the flour, baking powder, baking soda, and nutmeg. Cut the butter into the dry ingredients with a pastry blender or two knives until it resembles coarse meal.

In another bowl, beat the eggs and add the sugar, milk, and vanilla. Beat well to dissolve the sugar. Add to the dough and mix very well until smooth. Wrap the dough in plastic wrap and refrigerate for at least 45 minutes or overnight.

Preheat the oven to 375°F.

Roll out the dough to about a 2-inch thickness and cut into shapes with plain or decorative cookie cutters. Place on baking sheets and bake until just cooked and lightly browned, 8 to 12 minutes; timing will depend on the size of the cookies. If desired, sprinkle the cookies with colored sugar or other decorations before baking.

Makes about 4 dozen

TOFFEE BARS

2 cups all-purpose flour
¼ teaspoon salt
½ pound (2 sticks) unsalted butter, softened
1 cup firmly packed light brown sugar
1 large egg yolk
1 teaspoon vanilla extract
8 ounces semisweet chocolate, cut into bits and melted
½ cup coarsely chopped pecans

Preheat the oven to 350°F. Butter a baking pan that measures 9 x 12 inches or smaller.

In a bowl, sift together the flour and salt. Add the butter and sugar and mix well. Add the egg yolk and vanilla and mix very well.

Using your fingers, press the dough into the prepared pan, making a thin, even layer. Bake for 10 minutes.

While the dough is still warm, spread the top with the melted chocolate and sprinkle with the nuts. When cool, cut into 1½ x 2-inch bars.

Makes about 3 dozen

Antique cookie molds stored in a chestnut buffet remain serviceable for the modern holiday baker.

CHRIS MEAD

FLORIDA TO ESCAPE THE COLD

Hand-painted plate reflects the brilliant colors of the tropics and exotic local specialties such as stone crab and conch.

MENU

*Chilled Stone Crab Claws
with Mustard Sauce or
Red Cocktail Sauce*

Conch Fritters

*Sour Orange and
Lime Chicken*

*Watercress, Avocado, and
Orange Salad*

Key Lime Pie

Chilled Dry White Wine

New Year's Day Lunch at Dick Duane's

Key West, Florida

Key West, Florida, is always my place of choice for a post-Christmas getaway with the children. The town, with its turn-of-the-century Victorian architecture, is as soothing and comforting as the climate.

Dick Duane, a fellow New Yorker who shares my enthusiasm for the retreat, manages to spend ten days a month there. My most memorable visits have included New Year's Day luncheon at Dick's 1849 "conch house." Conch, the tough mollusk that abounds in the coral reefs off the Florida Keys, is also Key West's hybrid house style, combining fanciful Victorian flourishes with straightforward New England farmhouse simplicity. The architecture has landmark status on the National Register of Historic Places.

Dick's house sits in a tropical setting of orchids, bougainvillea, hibiscus, native Key lime, and Spanish lime trees. The fragrance of jasmine on the fresh salt air is intoxicating—a natural tonic for calming the nerves of harried city dwellers. On the brick patio that adjoins the walled pool, luncheon unfolds at a leisurely pace in the highly skilled hands of Dick's longtime cook,

Evangeline Washington.

Evangeline's own father cooked for Key West's most famous citizen, Ernest Hemingway, and she learned a great deal at her father's side in the writer's kitchen. Thanks to her Bahamian ancestry, Cuban, Caribbean, and Spanish culinary traditions are also evident in her cooking style.

"Evangeline really does all her cooking from her head," says Dick about the instinctive way the chef prepares local standards, such as this luncheon's stone crab claws, conch fritters, sour orange and lime chicken, and Key lime pie. Her menus are based on the freshest ingredients the day happens to bring her. "The neighbors will knock on the door with the day's catch," Dick relates. "It might be red snapper, conch, stone crabs, yellowtail, or lobster—whatever, that's what goes into the pot and on the table."

A particular shopper, Evangeline goes to her sources for local staples, such as plantains, a bananalike fruit that is used in Caribbean cooking. "She only brings home plantains of a certain ripeness, so that when they are sautéed, they develop a sugary sweetness that is

heavenly," says Dick. Evangeline even takes along her own pots and pans to cook with. And she guards her cooking secrets carefully. "If I come into the kitchen while she's cooking," says Dick, "she'll turn her back on me to keep her secrets to herself!"

However, there's no secret about the effect her cooking has on guests—it's the best way to start the new year.

Evangeline Washington serves up a luncheon that reflects her Bahamian ancestry. She learned Caribbean cooking from watching her father prepare meals for Key West's most illustrious resident, Ernest Hemingway. Dick Duane, a television producer and agent, is a frequent host in Key West.

Chris Mead

Locally caught stone crab claws (left) are served ice cold with a choice of sauces and plenty of lime wedges. The botanical place mat comes fresh from an Aralia tree in the lush backyard setting. The ordinary fritter (below) becomes sublime with the addition of fresh conch meat to the spicy batter, served on a platter with a marine theme.

CHILLED STONE CRAB CLAWS

If you're lucky enough to find them at your fish market, don't hesitate to buy stone crab claws when they're in season. They're sold precooked; Evangeline recommends serving them ice cold with these sauces. For appetizers, figure on about 2 crab claws per person, along with 2 conch fritters, and plenty of lime wedges.

MUSTARD SAUCE

2 cups sour cream
¼ cup mayonnaise
2 tablespoons Dijon mustard
Salt and freshly ground black pepper
to taste

In a bowl, combine all of the ingredients and mix well. Cover and chill for at least 1 hour before serving.

Makes about 2½ cups

RED COCKTAIL SAUCE

1 cup ketchup
1 tablespoon well-drained prepared white
horseradish
Fresh lime juice, preferably from Key
limes
Dash of Tabasco sauce

In a bowl, combine the ketchup with the horseradish and add the lime juice to taste (about 2 teaspoons should be enough). Add a dash of Tabasco for spiciness, cover, and refrigerate for 1 hour before serving.

Makes about 1 cup

CONCH FRITTERS

Don't miss conch fritters if you're ever in Key West—they're delicious.

1 pound fresh conch meat (or frozen, if
fresh is not available)
1 medium onion
½ sweet green pepper
3 garlic cloves
6 large eggs
¾ cup all-purpose flour
¼ cup milk
1½ teaspoons baking powder
1 teaspoon Tabasco sauce
Salt and freshly ground black pepper
Vegetable oil for frying

In a food processor, chop the conch meat until well ground. Set it aside in a mixing bowl.

Using the processor, finely chop the onion, sweet pepper, and garlic. Add the vegetables and mix well.

Beat the eggs until frothy. Add the eggs to the conch mixture and mix well.

Stir in the flour, milk, baking powder, Tabasco sauce, and salt and pepper to taste; blend well.

In a deep skillet or deep-fryer, heat at least 2 inches of oil until very hot. Drop the mixture by tablespoons into the oil and fry until golden brown on both sides. Drain well on paper towels before serving hot.

Serves 8

The historic architecture of Key West presents itself in such gems as this front-gabled folk Victorian house with a two-tiered porch and abundance of spindlework detail.

The addition of native limes and sour oranges to the marinade produces southern fried chicken with a local twist.

SOUR ORANGE AND LIME CHICKEN

Sour oranges are abundant in Key West but seldom seen elsewhere. If you can't get them at your store, substitute a mixture of half fresh orange juice and half fresh lemon juice. If you can't find Key limes, substitute half fresh lime juice and half lemon juice.

2 to 3 chickens, 3½ to 4½ pounds each, cut up for frying

1 garlic bulb, separated into cloves and minced or crushed

1⅓ cups fresh sour orange juice plus ⅔ cup Key Lime juice, or ⅔ cup fresh orange juice plus 1 cup fresh lemon juice plus ⅓ cup fresh lime juice

2 tablespoons freshly ground black pepper, at least

Vegetable oil for frying

2 large eggs

½ cup milk

About 3 cups all-purpose flour

Wash and dry the chicken pieces. Place them in a nonreactive bowl or dish and add the garlic, fruit juices, and pepper. Toss carefully to coat the chicken with the marinade; cover and refrigerate overnight.

Heat a generous quantity of oil until very hot in a deep skillet or deep-fryer.

Meanwhile, in a shallow bowl, beat the eggs with the milk until frothy. Place the flour in another shallow bowl.

Dip the chicken, one piece at a time, first into the egg and then into the flour, shaking off any excess but making sure the chicken is well coated.

Fry the chicken in the hot oil until dark golden brown. Drain on paper towels and serve.

Serves 8

WATERCRESS, AVOCADO, AND ORANGE SALAD

The colorful salad is topped with a creamy cooling dressing with interesting flavors.

DRESSING

½ cup fresh orange juice

3 tablespoons raspberry vinegar

2 teaspoons mayonnaise

½ teaspoon sugar

1 cup sour cream

SALAD

3 bunches fresh watercress, washed and dried

6 large navel oranges

1 large ripe avocado

Make the dressing: In a bowl, whisk together the orange juice, vinegar, mayonnaise, and sugar until the sugar has dissolved. Add the sour cream and beat until smooth. Cover and refrigerate for at least 1 hour.

To serve, break up the watercress and spread it over a large platter or on individual salad plates.

Peel the oranges and slice them into rounds. Arrange the slices at intervals over the watercress.

Peel and pit the avocado and slice it into thin crescents. Arrange the slices between the orange rounds. Serve with salad dressing drizzled over or passed separately.

Serves 8

A coconut tree, with its fruit (left), is a picturesque reminder of the town's tropical location.
A hibiscus blossom is the center of a salad (right) featuring avocado and orange picked in the yard.

CHRIS MEAD

KEY LIME PIE

The crust is different from most graham cracker crusts—much firmer, more cookielike, and very crunchy. Make the pie a day ahead of time and serve it ice cold.

CRUST

> 1½ **cups crushed graham crackers**
>
> 8 **tablespoons (1 stick) unsalted butter, very well softened**
>
> ½ **cup sugar**

FILLING

> 3 **large eggs, separated and at room temperature**
>
> 1 **14-ounce can sweetened condensed milk**
>
> ½ **cup Key lime juice plus the juice of 1 lemon, or** ⅓ **cup fresh lime juice plus** ⅓ **cup fresh lemon juice**
>
> 1 **cup sugar**

Preheat the oven to 375°F.

Make the crust: Combine the graham cracker crumbs, butter, and sugar until well mixed. Evenly press the mixture into a 9-inch pie plate.

Bake for 5 to 7 minutes, or until slightly browned. Set the crust aside to cool and lower the oven to 350°F.

Make the filling: In a bowl, whisk together the egg yolks, sweetened condensed milk, and fruit juices until completely smooth. Taste the filling; if it is not tart, add more lemon or lime juice.

Pour the filling into the piecrust and bake in the hot oven for about 15 minutes while you make the meringue.

In a bowl, beat the egg whites until soft peaks form. Begin adding the 1 cup of sugar, a tablespoon or two at a time, until stiff peaks form and all of the sugar is incorporated.

Spoon the meringue over the filling to cover it completely and continue baking just until the meringue is lightly browned, 20 to 30 minutes.

Remove the pie from the oven and cool to room temperature on a wire rack. Chill overnight before serving very cold.

Serves 8

Key lime pie (top), long identified with Key West, actually had its origins in the cuisine of nearby Cuba. A wooden building (above) is part of Key West's color; a Florida sunset (above right) is part of its romance. Sponges (right) dry below a sign proclaiming the southernness of the spot.

CHRIS MEAD

JANUARY IN CALIFORNIA

MENU

Black Caviar

*Water Biscuits or
Toast Triangles*

Sliced Cucumbers

Chopped Onion

Lemon Wedges

Sour Cream

Local Sausages

Local Cheese

*Schramsberg Cuvée de
Pinot Napa Valley
Champagne*

Napa Valley, California

A California sunset is one of the best light shows in the world, and natives of that state seem to appreciate what an appropriate backdrop it makes for bringing people together. I saw this firsthand when I got the loan of a cabin in the woods from some San Francisco friends.

Their log house stands on top of Mount Saint Helena at the end of a winding dirt road that was dug out of the mountain by Chinese laborers in the early 1900s. That work force had been imported to construct the stone buildings, still in use today, of the Christian Brothers Winery nearby.

Originally part of a ranch, the house has a screened porch with a breathtaking view of Napa Valley. Orange trees are close enough for their aroma to waft up to the porch. In the distance are towering stands of redwood trees, olive groves, and evergreens. Over all

is the dome of the sky, blue by day, streaked with brilliant hues of red, orange, and pink as the sun drops low into the horizon.

If you are fortunate enough to have a room with a special view, whether it looks out on a panorama of mountains, a stretch of water, a cityscape, or a simple garden, late afternoon tea or evening cocktails can be a rewarding and even magical experience.

On Mount Saint Helena, I offered friends well-chilled California rosé Champagne (what else!) and caviar. Even an inexpensive caviar—and I always keep a modest Romanoff variety in the pantry in case unexpected guests drop by—makes an elegant canapé when it is served with water biscuits or toast triangles. To serve with the caviar, I like to put out an assortment of garnishes in separate pottery crocks. I show guests how to "layer" the canapé—cracker, sour cream, cucumber, caviar, onion, and a squeeze of lemon—and pour the Champagne into tall crystal flutes. Then we all turn our attention to the view. After all, as I learned in California, sunsets are for watching.

*A screened porch with honey
rattan furniture from the 1930s
is dressed up by caviar,
Champagne, and a dazzling
panoramic view.*

Santa Monica, California

Nancy Goslee Power and I have been close friends since the fifth grade, when she came to one of my mother's dancing classes at the country club in Rehoboth Beach, Delaware. We learned how to be correct young ladies and to waltz. If we weren't at each other's weekend houses, then we were probably at the movies. We saw *Seven Brides for Seven Brothers* together seven times and that alone probably made us friends for life.

Fortunately, I'm in southern California frequently enough to enjoy long visits with Nancy and to sample the local cooking she likes to serve alfresco. "I can't wait for balmy weather so we can have Sunday lunch outside or cook in the fireplace and dance by the moon," says Nancy about the Italian-inspired courtyard that is the gathering place of choice in her Santa Monica, California, home.

The courtyard came with the house that Nancy and film producer Derek Power moved into after their marriage several years ago, and it completely changed her ideas

about entertaining. "It made me give up formal dinner parties and concentrate on occasions that were more in tune with the natural world around us," she says. "We gave a full-moon party one year, for example. Everyone wore white, the courtyard was lit only by candles and moonlight, and we all danced."

Nancy's theatrical approach to entertaining is inherited. Her mother "really staged an event when she entertained. She had a luau before anyone ever knew what one was. Dinner parties had to be dramatic and have impact. For her that was more fun than the food." Nancy is the same. "I enjoy building a mood. I also like seating eleven or twelve people at a table for

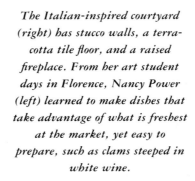

The Italian-inspired courtyard (right) has stucco walls, a terra-cotta tile floor, and a raised fireplace. From her art student days in Florence, Nancy Power (left) learned to make dishes that take advantage of what is freshest at the market, yet easy to prepare, such as clams steeped in white wine.

MENU

*Steamed Clams or
New Zealand Green
Mussels in Broth*

*Grilled White Sea Bass
with Wild Fennel*

Buttered New Potatoes

*Green Beans with
Chanterelles or
Artichokes with Salsa and
Cilantro*

Italian Bread

Japanese Persimmons

Fresh California Walnuts

California Chardonnay

eight. Cramming in more people than the table is supposed to hold makes everyone chummy!"

A frequent entertainer, Nancy describes her personal cooking style as "Tidewater-Italian-Californian," which, roughly translated, means lots of seafood prepared with Mediterranean techniques and the freshest California ingredients. She loves to forage for greens, such as wild fennel, which grows profusely nearby. "I learned this from our cook when I was a child; she would take me out to the woods with her when she went hunting for field greens." Her Italian tastes are the result of two years spent abroad at art school in Florence. "At the time I was living on a hundred and fifty dollars a month," she recalls, "but I managed to put enough aside to hire a maid for a few hours a week. I did it not so much for the cleaning, but to learn how to

cook authentic dishes from a native!"

Southern California weather permits Nancy to "stage" her events in the walled courtyard and to show off her skills as a professional garden designer specializing in English gardens for a Mediterranean-type climate. The profusion of blooms includes bougainvillea in vivid oranges, yellows, and white, bauhinia vine, a flower that looks like a yellow geranium, and a climbing rose called Mermaid, a creamy yellow flower that is standard in England as well as in Provence.

The courtyard is not used solely for gala events. Nancy and her husband retreat there every evening to enjoy a glass of wine or a Margarita before dinner, oftentimes in front of a fire to ward off the chill. Just beyond the courtyard is a "secret garden," a pocket-size oasis where Nancy takes her afternoon tea and delights in a

quiet time, a tradition that has been with her since childhood. "Mother would always set aside a time for us to chat and read," she recalls. "We'd sit and talk and eat something exotic like anchovies and crackers. It was probably one of the highlights of my youth."

STEAMED CLAMS OR NEW ZEALAND GREEN MUSSELS IN BROTH

It's hard to stop eating these clams or mussels and the bread that's required for sopping up the broth. If you don't like clams and can't find New Zealand Greens, buy whatever mussels are available.

> 3 tablespoons unsalted butter
> 5 shallots, minced
> ½ cup minced fresh cilantro (coriander)
> 2 8-ounce bottles clam juice
> ½ cup dry white wine
> 2½ to 3 pounds clams or New Zealand green mussels, scrubbed and debearded
> Crusty Italian bread and lemon wedges for serving

In a large, heavy nonreactive saucepan, melt the butter over moderate heat. Add the shallots and sauté until they are translucent, 3 to 5 minutes.

Add the cilantro, clam juice, wine, and clams or mussels. Cover and steam until the clams or mussels open, about 6 minutes. Discard any that do not open.

Serve the clams or mussels and broth in heated soup plates, accompanied by crusty Italian bread and lemon wedges.

Serves 2

Unexpected combinations are trademarks of the cook, whether she's mixing her china patterns or adding an herb like cilantro to sharpen a first course of steamed clams.

Ingredients for a supper highlighting California cuisine are laid out on a weathered pine table. The sea bass, stuffed with fresh fennel and scallions and tied with fragrant olive branches, will be grilled in the fireplace.

GRILLED WHITE SEA BASS WITH WILD FENNEL

Nancy Power has the good fortune to live where olive tree twigs are widely available. If you have the same good fortune, tie the fish as she does, between olive branches, and bind it with raffia. If not, use a wire fish grill.

1 3- to 4-pound white sea bass, salmon, lingcod, or other oily fish that is appropriate for grilling

About ½ cup chopped wild fennel or domestic fennel tops

¼ to ½ cup chopped scallions

Clarified unsalted butter or virgin olive oil for basting

Wash the fish, and pat it dry, inside and out, with paper towels.

Stuff the cavity with the fennel and scallions. Fashion a fish grill from olive branches or use a wire one and place the fish in it.

Prepare a grill with plenty of charcoal. When the coals are glowing and ash covered, add soaked dried fennel stalks, if available. (Dried fennel imported from France is available at many specialty shops.)

Grill the fish, basting frequently, for 10 minutes per inch of thickness (measured at the thickest point), until it is just barely opaque and flaky. Do not overcook; take care to baste the fish frequently with butter or oil.

Cut the fish into fillets or steaks and accompany with new potatoes cooked in their jackets and buttered just before serving.

Serves 4 to 6

An oversize Mexican plate holds grilled sea bass, new potatoes tossed in butter, and green beans served with locally grown chanterelle mushrooms.

GREEN BEANS WITH CHANTERELLES

Fresh green beans and fresh chanterelles from the Santa Monica Mountains tossed with butter pair perfectly with grilled fish and tiny new potatoes.

1 pound small fresh green beans

6 tablespoons (¾ stick) unsalted butter

¼ to ½ pound fresh Santa Monica Mountain chanterelles or other fresh chanterelles

Salt and freshly ground black pepper

Trim the beans; if not very small, halve or quarter them lengthwise.

Steam the beans until just crisp-tender.

Meanwhile, in a large skillet, melt the butter over moderate heat. Add the mushrooms and sauté just until limp. Add the beans and toss with the butter and mushrooms. Serve at once.

Serves 2

ARTICHOKES WITH SALSA AND CILANTRO

2 artichokes, trimmed

Juice of ½ lemon

1 cup homemade or store-bought salsa (page 92)

¼ cup chopped chick-peas

2 garlic cloves, minced

⅓ cup minced fresh cilantro (coriander)

2 teaspoons fresh lemon juice

Salt and freshly ground black pepper

Boil or steam the artichokes until tender; then cut out the chokes. Rub the cut portion with the juice of ½ lemon to prevent discoloration.

In a bowl, combine the salsa with the chick-peas, garlic, cilantro, lemon juice, and salt and pepper to taste. The mixture should have some bite; add more lemon juice or cilantro if needed.

Spoon the salsa mixture into the centers of the artichokes and serve.

Serves 2

On a cutting board with a cutout
heart (left), artichokes have been
tied and clipped, ready for
steaming. This California
standard will be served cool, filled
with a spicy salsa for dipping the
leaves. Left to ripen on a sunny
sill, Japanese persimmons (below)
in the straw-wrapped compote
will be the healthful dessert course.

SIMPLE PASTA DINNER
AT SUDIE WOODSON'S

✢✢✢✢✢✢✢

Saint Helena, California

Every Friday evening Sudie Woodson leaves her interior design business and house in San Francisco, California, behind and hops in the car with her two children. She says she can't imagine not making the ninety-minute drive each weekend to be in her "escape house" in the Napa Valley.

I immediately saw why when I visited her there. Her unpretentious ranch-style house in Saint Helena overlooks forty sunbathed slopes of cultivated vineyards belonging to the Christian Brothers and Krug wineries. Her own property is thickly planted with peach and apple trees, persimmons, fig trees, and a vegetable garden. She also raises twenty varieties of table grapes and sixty varieties of Zinfandel wine grapes.

The house is comfortably furnished with odds and ends that are well suited to the life-style of this semirural area. "I don't keep fancy china and crystal up here," Sudie notes. She prefers to use assorted green spongeware bowls and mottled green plates from the 1930s and 1940s.

The kitchen features an old six-burner gas stove Sudie's grandmother might have used, but her cooking style is very much up to date, reflecting the traditions of Napa Valley, with its plethora of excellent restaurants and food shops.

Typically, Saturday unwinds at a leisurely pace, starting with a morning walk through the property and a look at the garden to see what is ready for harvesting. After her stroll, Sudie will call local friends to catch up on the news and gossip, and invite folks for dinner. She never knows exactly how many people will show up. "Sometimes it gets to be a crowd. That's why, for the main course, I'll usually serve a pasta, because that allows me to add or subtract portions until the last minute," Sudie explains. "A more ambitious dinner would make everything too complicated, and relaxing is what a weekend in the country is all about."

✢✢✢✢✢✢✢

On a painted enamel kitchen table, dinnerware from the 1930s and 1940s is used for casual weekend entertaining in the Napa Valley.

MENU

*Capelli with Fresh
Tomato Sauce*

*Red and Green Salad with
Basil Vinaigrette*

*Onion and Sesame
Bagel Sticks*

Fresh Figs

*Bunches of
Zinfandel Grapes*

*Homegrown English
Walnuts*

Chocolate Swirl Cake

California Wines

The menu is dictated by what's at the peak of ripeness in the garden: fresh tomato sauce for angel's hair pasta and two-green salad to be served family style from a country platter and bowl.

CAPELLI WITH FRESH TOMATO SAUCE

When tomatoes are at their best, you'll be tempted to make this sauce nightly.

- 10 large ripe tomatoes
- ¼ cup olive oil
- 5 garlic cloves, minced
- 3 tablespoons chopped fresh basil
- 1 tablespoon chopped fresh parsley
- 1 cup heavy cream
  Salt and freshly ground black pepper
- 1¼ pounds fresh capelli (angel's hair) pasta
- ½ cup freshly grated Parmesan cheese

Peel, seed, and finely chop the tomatoes, reserving the juice.

In a large nonreactive skillet, warm the olive oil over moderate heat. Add the garlic and sauté for 2 to 3 minutes, or until fragrant and golden.

Stir in the tomatoes, basil, and parsley. Turn the heat to moderately low and cook, stirring from time to time, for 15 to 20 minutes.

Add the cream to the tomato sauce and stir to combine. Season with salt and pepper to taste and cook for 1 to 2 minutes, or until heated through.

In a large pot of salted boiling water, cook the capelli until just *al dente,* 1 to 2 minutes after the water returns to a boil. Drain and turn onto a warm serving platter.

Stir the Parmesan cheese into the sauce to thicken it. Spoon the sauce over the pasta and serve hot, accompanied by additional Parmesan cheese.

Serves 4

━━━━━━━━━━━━━━━━

RED AND GREEN SALAD WITH BASIL VINAIGRETTE

SALAD

1 large head buttercrunch or Boston lettuce

2 small heads radicchio

12 to 16 Calamata or other Greek olives

¼ to ½ pound feta cheese, cubed or crumbled

BASIL VINAIGRETTE

½ cup olive oil

3 tablespoons red or white wine vinegar

Juice of ½ large lemon

1 tablespoon Dijon mustard

1 tablespoon chopped fresh basil

1 garlic clove, minced

Salt and freshly ground black pepper

Wash and dry the lettuce. Arrange the leaves in a salad bowl and sprinkle with the olives and feta cheese.

In a jar, combine all of the vinaigrette ingredients, seasoning with salt and pepper to taste. Cover and shake well. Dress the salad immediately before serving.

Serves 4

━━━━━━━━━━━━━━━━

CHOCOLATE SWIRL CAKE

½ pound (2 sticks) unsalted butter, softened

½ cup shortening

3 cups sugar

6 large eggs, at room temperature

1 cup milk

3 cups plus 1 tablespoon all-purpose flour

½ teaspoon baking powder

2 teaspoons vanilla extract

1 teaspoon brandy

1 cup semisweet chocolate chips, melted and cooled

Preheat the oven to 275°F. Butter and flour a large tube pan.

In a large bowl, cream together the butter, shortening, and sugar with an electric mixer. One at a time, add the eggs, beating until incorporated before adding the next one.

Add the milk, flour, and baking powder and beat until the batter is smooth and light. Add the vanilla and brandy and incorporate.

In a small bowl, combine 1 cup of the batter with the melted chocolate chips and mix well.

Pour the white cake batter into the prepared pan and add the chocolate batter. Using a table knife or skewer, swirl the chocolate batter into the white batter to marbelize.

Place the pan on a baking sheet and bake in the center of the oven for 2 to 2¼ hours, or until a toothpick inserted in the center comes out clean.

Allow the cake to cool in the pan on a wire rack. Unmold and cut into thin slices to serve with fresh figs, Zinfandel grapes, and fresh walnuts.

Serves 12

━━━━━━━━━━━━━━━━

On an old pizza baking board, homegrown figs, Zinfandel grapes, English walnuts, and chocolate swirl cake offer a choice of desserts in a sumptuous still-life setting.

LATE WINTER IN TENNESSEE

Nashville, Tennessee

Since the first Heart of Country show in 1982, this annual event for collectors and dealers (above) has confirmed the Country look as a nationwide phenomenon. Even the Nashville taxis pay homage to the lyrical traditions of Music City (top).

My February calendar would be incomplete without a big red heart encircling the dates for the Heart of Country Antiques Show in Nashville, Tennessee. It was here, in 1982, that my good friends Libby and Richard Kramer first presented the event that would become known as "the show that captured America's heart."

American Country had recently been published when I was invited to participate as a special guest, an appearance that would seal for me so many friendships north and south, east and west. From forty-two states, hundreds of dealers and collectors came to a gathering that was more like a family reunion than a business occasion. "This was the first show that brought together everyone interested in collecting Country antiques in much the same way that Mary's first book did. For all of us, it was the beginning of a Country network," explains Libby.

I look forward to Heart of Country every year as much for the excitement

of the shopping as for the cooking that highlights the Preview Party. For the show's fifth anniversary, there was a smorgasbord of southern food that just about upstaged the antiques.

Platters were piled high with regional specialties like "mock oysters," a cornmeal recipe that has endured since Civil War days, and Tennessee smoked ham and turkey along with family favorites like Libby Kramer's rice muffins with stewed apricot jam and pride-of-Tennessee smoked turkeys and hams. Of course, no Country table would be complete without desserts and there were many to choose from, including old-fashioned chess pie squares and the Nashville candy product called Goo Goo Bars, which are as famous as the city's legendary country music stars.

The recipes prepared for the Heart of Country Show are family standards that have been passed down through generations; they are a sampler of regional riches and ingenuity.

MENU

Mint Juleps

Crudités

*Black-Eyed Pea Dip with
Benne (Sesame) Crackers*

Mock Oysters

Tennessee Ham

Smoked Tennessee Turkeys

Brown-Sugar Bacon

Baked Potato Skins

Dollar Rolls

Rice Muffins

Corn Sticks

Stewed Apricot Jam

Jack Daniel's Squares

Chess Pie

Fresh Fruit

*Humble farm staples of bacon,
potatoes, and corn have been
transformed into brown-sugar
bacon, baked potato skins, and
corn fritters that taste like fried
oysters. The corn-bread sticks
were baked in a mold.*

MINT JULEPS

This is a drink that makes the day pass at a genuine southern pace.

- 3 to 4 fresh mint leaves
- 1 teaspoon superfine sugar
- 2 tablespoons club soda or seltzer
  Crushed ice
- 2 ounces bourbon or sour mash whiskey
  Fresh mint sprigs for garnish

In the bottom of a chilled glass, bruise the mint leaves with a long-handled spoon. Add the sugar and club soda and stir to dissolve the sugar and mix it with the mint.

Fill the glass to the rim with crushed ice and pour the bourbon over. Garnish with mint sprigs and drink up.

Makes 1 serving

BLACK-EYED PEA DIP

Serve this dip the traditional way—with benne wafers (otherwise known as sesame crackers).

- 1 10-ounce package frozen black-eyed peas, or ⅔ cup dried black-eyed peas, soaked overnight
- 8 bacon slices
- ½ cup finely chopped onion
- 2 cups sour cream
- 2 teaspoons fresh lemon juice
  Salt and freshly ground black pepper

In a skillet or saucepan, combine the peas with 2 slices of the bacon and add water to cover. Bring to a boil over high heat; turn the heat to low and simmer for 1 hour.

Meanwhile, fry the remaining 6 slices of bacon. Drain on paper towels, crumble, and set aside.

Strain the peas and bacon, reserving the cooking liquid; discard the bacon.

Put the peas and 2 tablespoons of the reserved liquid in a food processor and purée. Add more liquid, as needed, and process until the peas are puréed and smooth; the mixture should be thick but not runny.

Scrape the purée into a bowl and stir in the crumbled bacon, onion, sour cream, lemon juice, and salt and pepper to taste.

Serve cold or at room temperature, garnished with additional crumbled bacon, if desired.

Makes about 3 cups

MOCK OYSTERS

A dish that dates back to the Civil War, these small corn fritters actually look and—somehow—taste like fried oysters.

- 1 cup fresh or frozen corn
- 1 large egg, beaten
- ¼ cup milk
- 2 tablespoons unsalted butter, melted
- ½ teaspoon salt
  Pinch of lemon pepper
- ⅔ cup all-purpose flour
  Vegetable oil for frying

In a bowl, combine the corn, egg, milk, butter, salt, and lemon pepper. Add the flour and mix well; the batter will be very thick and sticky.

In a large skillet or deep-fryer, heat the oil until very hot. Drop the batter by tablespoons into the hot oil and deep-fry until golden brown on all sides. Drain on paper towels and serve hot.

Makes 8 fritters

Buffet plate offers dollar roll sandwiches, seasonal fruits, and vegetables for dipping in sour cream enlivened with puréed black-eyed peas and bacon.

DOLLAR ROLLS

These dollar-size biscuits are flaky and tender. They can be cut out ahead of time and frozen until needed. Then just bake them—the results will be perfect.

2 cups milk, scalded and cooled to lukewarm

1 tablespoon active dry yeast

¼ cup sugar

About 2½ cups all-purpose flour

8 tablespoons (1 stick) unsalted butter, melted

1 tablespoon baking powder

½ teaspoon baking soda

½ teaspoon salt

In a bowl, combine the lukewarm milk with the yeast and sugar and set aside to proof for a few minutes, until foamy.

Stir in about 2 cups of the flour, or enough to make the batter resemble the consistency of pancake batter. Set aside in a warm place to rise until doubled.

Preheat the oven to 400°F. Grease two baking sheets.

Stir the dough to deflate it and add about ½ cup of flour along with the butter, baking powder, baking soda, and salt. Mix well. The dough should be somewhat heavy yet airy; if it seems lighter or "thinner" than biscuit dough, add more flour as needed.

Roll out the dough to a ½-inch thickness and cut into silver dollar-size rounds with a biscuit cutter.

Place the biscuits on the prepared baking sheets and bake for 10 to 15 minutes, or until browned.

Makes about 3 dozen

Gabled roofs distinguish a charming collection of rustic residences for birds (above left). Crafts and antiques are exhibited by dealers (above) from over 40 states at the Heart of Country show. At the preview party the comforts of good food are sought by antiques exhibitors and collectors (below).

RICE MUFFINS

Amazingly similar in texture to English crumpets, rice muffins are delicious with melted butter and homemade preserves.

 2 to 3 tablespoons shortening, melted
 1 large egg
 1 cup milk
 1 cup cooked white rice
 1 cup all-purpose flour, sifted
 2 teaspoons baking powder
 1 teaspoon sugar
 ¼ teaspoon salt

Preheat the oven to 450°F.

Using the melted shortening, very generously grease a 12-cup muffin tin.

In a bowl, whisk together the egg and milk. Stir in the rice. Sift together the flour, baking powder, sugar, and salt and add the dry ingredients to the rice mixture. Stir to mix very well.

Divide the batter among the greased muffin cups and bake for about 15 minutes, or until lightly browned on top.

Makes 1 dozen

STEWED APRICOT JAM

This quick, easy jam is delicious on dollar rolls or rice muffins.

 ½ pound dried apricots
 ¾ cup sugar

Wash the apricots and remove any stems. Place them in a heavy saucepan and add water to cover. Bring to a boil over high heat; turn the heat to low and simmer, uncovered, until the apricots are plump and tender.

Add the sugar and stir until it has completely dissolved. Cook for 10 minutes more, taking care that the mixture doesn't scorch.

Turn the mixture into a blender or food processor and purée to the consistency you desire. Serve as a jam on Dollar Rolls or Rice Muffins.

Makes about 1½ cups

The first flowers of spring bloom in profusion (left), especially colorful when set against a backdrop of Tennessee quilts.

JACK DANIEL'S SQUARES

These bourbon-spiked "brownies" make a spiritous addition to the dessert table.

SQUARES

> 2 cups granulated sugar
> 1 cup chopped pecans
> ½ cup all-purpose flour
> ½ cup unsweetened cocoa powder
> 3 large eggs
> 3 tablespoons Jack Daniel's whiskey
> 1 teaspoon vanilla extract
> ½ pound (2 sticks) unsalted butter, melted

ICING

> 1 cup confectioners' sugar
> 1 1-ounce square unsweetened chocolate, melted and cooled
> 1 tablespoon unsalted butter, softened
> 1 tablespoon Jack Daniel's whiskey
> 1 tablespoon milk
> 1 teaspoon vanilla extract

Make the squares: Preheat the oven to 350°F. Butter a 9-inch square baking pan.

In a bowl, combine the granulated sugar, pecans, flour, and cocoa and stir until thoroughly mixed. Add the eggs, whiskey, vanilla, and melted butter and mix until smooth.

Pour the batter into the prepared pan and bake in the center of the oven for 45 minutes. Let cool to room temperature on a wire rack.

Make the icing: In a bowl, combine the confectioners' sugar, chocolate, butter, whiskey, milk, and vanilla and beat with a wooden spoon until smooth and spreadable. If the icing is too thick, add more milk, a teaspoon at a time.

Coat the tops of the squares with the icing and serve cold or at room temperature.

Makes 12 to 16 squares

CHESS PIE

Don't cut huge wedges of the pie until you've tasted it. It's so rich, a pie this size may just serve a crowd.

> 2⅓ cups firmly packed light brown sugar
> 3 large eggs
> ½ cup heavy cream
> 1½ teaspoons vanilla extract
> ½ teaspoon salt
> 4 tablespoons (½ stick) unsalted butter, melted
> 1 9-inch unbaked pie shell (page 72)

Preheat the oven to 325°F.

In a bowl, combine the brown sugar, eggs, cream, vanilla, salt, and butter and stir or beat until thoroughly mixed.

Place the pie shell on a baking sheet and pour the filling into it. Bake for 1 hour, or until the filling is puffed on top and bubbling around the edges. Let cool to room temperature on a wire rack before serving.

Serves 6 to 8

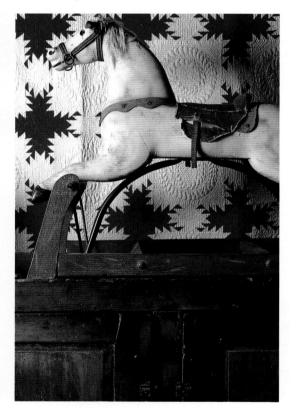

Whether in the carved details of a rocking horse or the millions of stitches required to produce a finished quilt, the unknown folk artist is the real star of the show.

Finale to the evening's meal includes this trio of regional favorites: chess pie wedge, Jack Daniel's brownie, and shortbread cookie heart.

*Mary Emmerling stands by a
heart of flowers at the
antiques show.*

DIRECTORY OF FOOD SOURCES

This nationwide guide provides listings for retail stores and mail-order sources specializing in high-quality foods ranging from fresh produce, baked goods, and jams and jellies to smoked meats and other regional specialties.

ALABAMA

PRIESTER'S PECANS
227 Old Fort Dr.
Fort Deposit, AL 36032
205-227-4301
Pecan halves and pieces, finely ground pecan meal, and roasted, salted pecan halves. Milk chocolate and white chocolate for baking and candy-making also available at retail shop.

JOE WILLIAMS PECANS
P.O. Box 640
Camden, AL 36726
205-682-4559
Shelled pecans, whole halves or large pieces, available from November through August.

ALASKA

ALASKA WILD BERRY PRODUCTS
528 East Pioneer Ave.
Homer, AK 99603
907-235-8858
Mail-order gifts of Alaskan canned salmon and meats as well as local wild berry jams, jellies, and sauces. Mail-order catalog.

ARIZONA

T & G PARADISE ACRES
855 East Main St.
Cottonwood, AZ 86326
602-634-5424
Mesquite for grilling and barbecuing.

ARKANSAS

OZARK MOUNTAIN SMOKE HOUSE
P.O. Box 37
Farmington, AR 72730
501-267-3339, 1-800-643-3437; in Arkansas 1-800-632-0155
Sugar-cured hickory- and sassafras-smoked ham, turkey, pork, bacon, chicken, sausages, and salamis. Also mustard, mustard ham glaze, and assorted jams and preserves.

CALIFORNIA

ALMOND PLAZA
P.O. Box 500
1701 C St.
Sacramento, CA 95803–9988
916-446-2500; 1-800-225-NUTS
Almonds and related baking ingredients. Call for free brochure and recipes.

CALIFORNIA KIWI PRODUCTS
680 Jones St.
Yuba City, CA 95991
916-673-8053
Kiwi fruit drink available in 32-ounce bottles.

CALIFORNIA SUNSHINE FINE FOODS, INC.
144 King St.
San Francisco, CA 94107
415-543-3007
Fresh specialty produce, domestic and imported caviars, smoked and fresh seafoods and game birds, American and imported game meat, exotic mushrooms.

CAVIAR EXPRESS
860 South Winchester Blvd.
San Jose, CA 95128
408-985-7444
Black Malossol Russian beluga.

DAISYFRESH DAIRY CULTURES
P.O. Box 36
Santa Cruz, CA 95063
408-427-3071
Yogurt, Danish sour cream, Swiss acidophilus, Irish buttermilk, dairy cultures; each tested for home use, directions and recipes included.

DEER CREEK WILD RICE
680 Jones St.
Yuba City, CA 95991
916-673-8053
California wild rice. Also available, a blend of wild rice and brown rice, and gift packs.

FANTASIA BAKERY
3465 California St.
San Francisco, CA 94118
415-752-0825
European bakery and confections. Specializing in wedding and birthday cakes.

FRED'S CHIPS
1500 Park Ave.
Emeryville, CA 94608
415-655-2196
Chips made from a blend of domestic and imported chocolates.

HANDAL'S DRY GOODS
256 South Robertson Blvd.
Beverly Hills, CA 90211
213-854-7286
Imported coffees and teas and an assortment of candies, coffeeware, and gift baskets. Mail order only.

J & K TRADING COMPANY
10808 Garland Dr.
Culver City, CA 90230
213-836-3334
Escargots, caviar, mushrooms, spices, and other delicacies.

LE BELGE CHOCOLATIER
P.O. Box 831
San Rafael, CA 94915
415-459-6220
Fresh, handmade Belgian molded chocolates.

LINDY'S MEXICAN PRODUCTS
P.O. Box 1142
San Bernardino, CA 92402
714-889-1956
Taco sauce and green taco salsa; free booklet of Mexican recipes available.

McFADDEN FARM
Potter Valley, CA 95469
707-743-1122
Garlic braids, bay leaf wreaths, grapevine wreaths, and California wild rice.

MAGIC EMERALD GLAZED PECANS
16 California St., Suite 505
San Francisco, CA 94111
415-562-2150
Glazed pecans and pecan halves dipped in praline made from natural products.

MAGIC GARDEN HERB COMPANY
Dept. A, P.O. Box 332
Fairfax, CA 94930
415-488-4331
Botanical and culinary herbs and spices. Also available are herbal teas and potpourri.

MAHOGANY SMOKED MEATS
MEADOW FARMS COUNTRY SMOKEHOUSE
P.O. Box 1387
Bishop, CA 93514
619-873-5311
Mahogany wood-smoked meats and poultry. Also available are smoked Cheddar cheese, raw sage honey, and Sierra pine nuts.

Moon Shine Trading Co.
P.O. Box 896
Winters, CA 95694
916-795-2092
Orange blossom, black button sage, yellow star thistle, eucalyptus, sunflower, clover, and other gourmet honeys. Butters and spreads, including almond butter, cashew butter, and halvah spread.

Napa Valley Mustard Co.
939 Oakville Crossroad
Oakville, CA 94562
707-994-8330
California hot and sweet mustard, green chili, garlic mustard, and country ketchup. Aprons and pot holders with the company logo. Gift packs are available.

Nature's Herb Company
281 Ellis St.
San Francisco, CA 94102
415-373-2756
Natural herbs and spices.

Pannikin Coffee & Tea
645 G St.
San Diego, CA 92101
619-239-1257
Top-grade coffees and delicate teas and spices. Also a selection of accessories and gift ideas.

S. E. Rykoff & Company
P.O. Box 21467
Market Street Station
Los Angeles, CA 90021
213-624-6094
Full line of spices in 1-pound containers, as well as foods and cookware previously only available to chefs and restaurants.

Nick Sciabica & Sons
P.O. Box 1246
Modesto, CA 95353
209-577-5067
One hundred percent pure, cold-pressed California virgin olive oil. Write for catalog and free recipes.

Sonoma Cheese Factory
2 Spain St., On the Plaza
Sonoma, CA 95476
707-996-1000
Makers of Sonoma Jack cheeses.

Taylor's Herb Garden, Inc.
1535 Lone Oak Rd.
Vista, CA 92084
619-727-3485
One hundred and thirty different varieties of herb plants and 180 varieties of herb seeds. Catalog: $1.

Gordon Thompson Ltd.
410 West Coast Highway
Newport Beach, CA 92663
714-645-5180
Catalog of wild game, exotic food, and recipes.

Timber Crest Farms
4791 Dry Creek Rd.
Healdsburg, CA 95448
707-433-8251
Dried fruits, dried tomatoes, nuts and candy, and gift packs.

Tsang and Ma
P.O. Box 294
Belmont, CA 94002
415-595-2270
Oriental specialty seasonings, sauces, flavored cooking and salad oils. Oriental cookware and a full line of Oriental vegetable seeds.

Valley Bakery
502 M St.
Fresno, CA 93721
209-485-2700
Creators of the original Valley Peda Bread and Valley Lahvosh. Specializing in heart-shaped crackers and baked goods.

Vanilla, Saffron Imports
70 Manchester St.
San Francisco, CA 94110
415-648-8990
Spanish saffron, vanilla beans and extracts, and dried wild mushrooms.

Wilda's Mustard
5133 Moon Shadow Ct.
Central Valley, CA 96019
916-275-6674
Specialty mustards.

Willacrik Farm
P.O. Box 599
Templeton, CA 93465
805-238-2276

Fresh giant elephant garlic: whole bulbs and cloves in bulk or gift packs, dehydrated chips, flakes, and powder. Also related gourmet items.

Williams-Sonoma
P.O. Box 7456
San Francisco, CA 94120–7456
415-652-9007
Everything for the cook, both equipment and ingredients.

COLORADO

High Valley Farm, Inc.
14 Alsace Way
Colorado Springs, CO 80906
303-634-2944
Cured and smoked meats and poultry and canned cocktail pâtés, including pheasant, trout, and turkey.

CONNECTICUT

Brae Beef
Stamford Town Center, Level 3
100 Greyrock Pl.
Stamford, CT 06901
203-323-4482; outside Connecticut
1-800-323-4484
All-natural beef, lamb, and turkey.

Capital Teas Ltd.
61 Dolan Dr.
Guilford, CT 06437
203-453-3761
Unblended single garden and straight provincial teas, flavored teas, and accessories.

Elizabeth Gallagher/Elizabeth's Best
P.O. Box 294
Mystic, CT 06355
203-599-3279; 203-536-6354
Home-baked shortbread, chocolate chip cookies, and coconut macaroons.

Matthews 1812 House, Inc.
Whitcomb Hill Rd.
Cornwall Bridge, CT 06754
203-672-6449
Specializing in homemade food and gifts, including Sunshine Lemon Rum Cake, Heritage Fruit & Nut Cake, and Heirloom Brandied Apricot Cake. Mail order only.

Stick to Your Ribs Texas Barbecue
1785 Stratford Ave.
Stratford, CT 06497
203-377-1752
Barbecued meats and chicken. Also barbecue sauce in four degrees of strength from mild to mean.

FLORIDA

Albritton Fruit Company, Inc.
5430 Proctor Rd.
Sarasota, FL 33583
813-923-2573
Citrus fruit and specialties, as well as mangoes and avocados.

Barfield Groves
P.O. Box 68
Polk City, FL 33868
813-984-1316
Fresh Florida citrus fruit.

Blue Heron Fruit Shippers, Inc.
7440 North Trail
Sarasota, FL 33580
813-355-6946; 1-800-237-3920
Fresh oranges, grapefruit, mangoes, and avocados.

Chalet Suzanne Foods, Inc.
P.O. Drawer A C
Lake Wales, FL 33859–9003
813-676-6011
Gourmet soups, sauces, and aspics.

Lee's Fruit Company
P.O. Box 2801
Leesburg, FL 32748
904-753-0555
Organic fruit, plant food, and compost.

Quail Roost Quail Farms, Inc.
8942 S.W. 129 Terrace
Miami, FL 33176
305-253-8319
Fresh dressed and frozen quail and pheasant.

St. James
P.O. Box 222800
Hollywood, FL 33022–2800
305-921-8882
Wisconsin Cheddars aged a minimum of 2 years.

GEORGIA

Exotica Brands, Inc.
P.O. Box 450134
Atlanta, GA 30345
404-496-0731
Brauhaus Beer Bread Mixes and a variety of bread mixes made without beer, such as Cola Bread and Yogurt/ Herb Bread. Send a self-addressed, stamped envelope for a free brochure.

Koinonia Products
Rt. 2
Americus, GA 31709
912-924-0391
Shelled, hand-sorted pecan halves and pieces, pecan specialty items, fruitcake, and peanuts.

Southern Cross Farms
P.O. Box 627
Vidalia, GA 30474
912-565-7880 in Georgia;
1-800-833-0009 outside Georgia
Vidalia sweet onions and specialty foods, including pecans and sweet potatoes.

SUNNYLAND FARMS, INC.
Willson Road at Pecan City
P.O. Box 549
Albany, GA 31703
912-883-3085
Pecans in the shell or shelled, natural or toasted. Also cashews, walnuts, almonds, pistachios, macadamias, peanuts, mixed nuts, and dried fruits.

HAWAII

ILI ILI FARM
Box 150
Kula, Maui, HI 96790
808-878-6230
Hawaiian fancy foods and exotic flowers, including Maui onions, macadamia nuts, and butters.

ILLINOIS

DEBORAH'S COUNTRY FRENCH BREAD
500 North Orleans St.
Chicago, IL 60610
312-321-6021
Crusty wheat bread from Poilâne's of Paris, France, baked in wood-fired ovens and flown anywhere in the United States.

THE ETHNIC PANTRY COMPANY
P.O. Box 798
Grayslake, IL 60030
312-223-6660
Hard-to-find spices, sauces, condiments, and flavorings. Mail order only. Free catalog available.

GOLDEN TROPHY STEAKS/DIVISION OF THE BRUSS CO.
3548 North Kostner Ave.
Chicago, IL 60641
312-282-2900
Specially selected cuts of meat.

HERBS NOW! THE GARDEN GOURMET
P.O. Box 775
Highland Park, IL 60035
312-432-7711
Fresh-cut herbs, exotic mushrooms, miniature vegetables, and imported fresh fruits and vegetables from Italy, France, and New Zealand.

KOLB-LENA CHEESE CO.
3990 Sunnyside Rd.
Lena, IL 61408
815-369-4577
Quality specialty cheeses. Mail-order catalog available.

MADAME CHOCOLATE, INC.
1940-C Lehigh Ave.
Glenview, IL 60025
312-729-3330
Bulk chocolate and chocolate gifts for the cook, baker, and candy-maker. Free catalog available. No shipments during summer months.

THE SHOPKEEPERS LTD.
1741 West 99th St.
Chicago, IL 60643
312-881-8400
Fruit fillings, jams, jellies, preserves, toppings, bakers' mixes, herbs, spices, coffee, tea, mustards, tapenade, tartines, fruit honeys, salad dressings, herbed vinegars, and syrups.

SIGNATURE PRIME MEATS
143 South Water Market
Chicago, IL 60608
312-829-0900; 1-800-621-0397
Gourmet meats, including lamb, pork, and veal, fowl, and seafood.

WESTDALE FOODS COMPANY
3245 West 111th St.
Chicago, IL 60655
312-238-3927
Specialty candy, chocolate, cookies, biscuits, preserves, and spices.

INDIANA

INDIANA BOTANIC GARDENS
P.O. Box 5
626 177 St.
Hammond, IN 46325
219-931-2480
Six hundred herbs, essential oils, herb seeds, and other natural products.

IOWA

AMANA SOCIETY MEAT MARKET
Amana, IA 52203
319-622-3111
Natural hickory-smoked hams and sausages and a variety of gourmet food items. Free catalog available.

THE GOURMET DAIRY
P.O. Box 714
Fairfield, IA 52556
515-472-8195
Clarified butter.

MAYTAG DAIRY FARMS
Box 806
Newton, IA 50208
515-792-1133
Maytag blue cheese, natural white Cheddar, Edam, regular yellow Cheddar, brick, and Swiss cheeses.

KENTUCKY

GETHSEMANI FARMS
Highway 247
Trappist, KY 40051
502-549-3117
Cheese and fruitcakes.

LOUISIANA

BAYOU BUFFET
P.O. Box 791127
New Orleans, LA 70179–1127
504-482-3752
Creole and Cajun seasonings, mixes, cookbooks, and kitchen equipment.

BAYOU FOOD PRODUCTS
1915 North Main
St. Martinville, LA 70582
318-394-5552
Cajun ethnic items unique to the St. Martinville area, including hot sauces, pickled peppers, okra, spices, and recipes.

CALHOUN PECAN SHELLING COMPANY
P.O. Box 784, Dept. ACC
Mansfield, LA 71052
318-872-2921
Fancy shelled pecan halves and cooking pieces in economy packs and decorative tins.

COMMUNITY KITCHENS
P.O. Box 3778
Baton Rouge, LA 70821–3778
1-800-535-9901
Special coffee blends of the region, Cajun spices, Creole seasonings, mixes, and gourmet teas.

CREOLE DELICACIES CO., INC.
533 Saint Ann St.
New Orleans, LA 70116
504-525-9508
Pecan pralines, praline topping, rémoulade sauce, hot pepper jelly, coffee and chicory, beignet mix, spices, preserves, soups, mustards, hot sauces, fruitcakes, smoked hams, turkeys, seasonings, cookbooks, and gift baskets.

EVANGELINE FOODS
P.O. Box 798
Banker Rd.
St. Martinville, LA 70582
318-394-3091
Hot sauces, pickled peppers, pepper sauces, long- and medium-grain rice, and Regent and Chinito brand rice.

GAZIN'S
2910 Toulouse St.
P.O. Box 19221
New Orleans, LA 70179
504-482-0302
Creole and Cajun foods and spices. Catalog: $1, refundable with first order.

ZATARAIN'S, INC.
82 First St.
P.O. Box 347
Gretna, LA 70053
504-367-2950
Breading, seasonings, and Creole specialties.

MAINE

CASPIAN CAVIARS
P.O. Box 876
Camden, ME 04843
207-236-8313; 207-236-4436
Caspian caviars, American sturgeon caviar, fresh salmon caviar, fresh pressed caviar, truffles and wild mushrooms, fresh and smoked poultry, game birds, fish and fresh game.

DOWNEAST SEAFOOD EXPRESS
Box 138
Brookville, ME 04617
800-556-2326
Overnight delivery of live lobsters as well as fresh crab meat, fresh lobster meat, shrimp, and sea scallops.

DUCKTRAP RIVER FISH FARM
R.F.D. #2, Box 378
Lincolnville, ME 04849
207-763-3960
Smoked Eastern and Western salmon and Maine smoked trout.

PORT CLYDE FOODS
P.O. Box 188
Rockland, ME 04841
207-594-4412
Fine gourmet canned seafood, including Holmes brand hand-packed Maine lobster and other specialty foods.

THE WHIP & SPOON
161 Commercial St.
P.O. Box 567
Portland, ME 04112
207-774-4020
A complete line of cookware, wine, food, cheese, and spices.

MARYLAND

BIG AL'S SEAFOOD MARKET
302 Talbot St.
Saint Michaels, MD 21663
301-745-2637
Big Al's own crab seasoning mix.

CHESAPEAKE SEAFOOD CATERERS
Rt. 1, Box 506
Saint Michaels, MD 21663
301-745-5056
Chesapeake Bay seafood, such as blue crab, oysters, blue crab meat, and soft-shell crabs.

CUSTARD COMPANY
4877 Battery Lane #32
Bethesda, MD 20814
301-652-9141
Coffee cakes and brownies made without preservatives, artificial colorings, or artificial flavorings.

ROY L. HOFFMAN & SONS
Rt. 6, Box 5
Hagerstown, MD 21740
301-739-2332
Country ham and bacon, smoked turkey, steaks, smoked pork chops, and smoked summer sausages.

MASSACHUSETTS

G. H. BENT CO.
7 Pleasant St.
Milton, MA 02186
617-698-5945
Common crackers and water crackers.

CATHERINE'S CHOCOLATES
R.D. 2, Box 32
Great Barrington, MA 02130
413-528-2410
Hand-dipped chocolates made from tradition-tested recipes.

THE COFFEE CONNECTION
342 Western Ave.
Brighton, MA 02135
617-254-1459
Twenty-three varieties of premium fresh-roasted coffees, 35 fine black and herbal teas, whole spices, vanilla beans, and bulk cocoa.

MARBLEHEAD LOBSTER COMPANY
Beacon and Orne Sts.
Marblehead, MA 01945
617-631-0787
Lobsters and fresh seafood native to New England.

NEW ENGLAND CHEESEMAKING SUPPLY COMPANY
Box 85
Ashfield, MA 01330
413-628-3808
Gourmet dairy food kits for cheese, butter, ice cream, and yogurt. Also beer, wine, and sausage kits. The company publishes a bimonthly newsletter for cheese-makers.

THE SOCIETY BAKERY
104 Charles St.
Box 877
Boston, MA 02114
617-648-4695
Fruitcake, sun-dried apricot cake, shortbread, and spiced pecans.

MICHIGAN

AMERICAN SPOON FOODS, INC.
411 East Lake St.
Petoskey, MI 49770
616-347-9030
Specializing in wild fruit preserves, such as wild blueberry, blackberry, grape, thimbleberry, and elderberry. Other items such as dried tart cherries, dried mushrooms, pickled wild leeks, vinegars, and mustards are also available.

FOX HILL FARM
Dept. 086-ACC, Box 7
Parma, MI 49269–0007
517-531-3179
Three hundred and fifty varieties of herbs available as plants, produce, or condiments. Catalog is $1.

WILDERNESS GOURMET
P.O. Box 3257
Ann Arbor, MI 48106
313-663-6987
Steaks, roasts, sausage, and wild game, such as venison, buffalo, wild boar, reindeer, goose, pheasant, partridge, and quail.

MINNESOTA

EICHTEN'S HIDDEN ACRES CHEESE FARM
16705 310 St.
Center City, MN 50512
612-257-4752
Raw milk cheeses, such as Gouda, baby Swiss, Colby, Tilsit, and Havarti.

NATURE'S BEST PREMIUM WILD RICE
P.O. Box 1362
Detroit Lakes, MN 56501–1362
218-847-3210
Premium wild rice in small or large-volume orders.

OAKWOOD GAME FARM
P.O. Box 274
Princeton, MN 55371
612-389-2077
Fresh and smoked game birds and other fine foods and gift items.

MISSISSIPPI

STERNBERG PECAN COMPANY
P.O. Box 193
Jackson, MS 39205
601-366-6310
Direct-mail sales of fresh shelled fancy mammoth pecan halves.

MISSOURI

MORNINGLAND DAIRY
Rt. 1, Box 188B
Mountain View, MO 65548
417-469-3817
Nine varieties of farm-made, raw milk cheese, including Cheddar, Monterey Jack, and Colby.

NEBRASKA

OMAHA STEAKS INTERNATIONAL
4400 South 96th St.
P.O. Box 3300
Omaha, NE 68103
800-228-9055
Specializing in hand-trimmed cuts of corn-fed, naturally aged midwestern beef. Catalog of steaks and other gourmet foods is available for $1.

NEW HAMPSHIRE

GLEN ECHO FARMS
Box 2
Wendell, NH 03782
603-863-6780
Producers of high-quality lambs and suppliers of other specialty foods.

HARMAN'S CHEESE & COUNTRY STORE
Sugar Hill, NH 03585
603-823-8000
Specializing in Cheddar cheese, aged naturally for at least two years. Also pure maple syrup and maple products, seedless preserves, smoked canned salmon, canned crab meat, the "cracker barrel" crackers, and other gourmet items. Brochure is free.

NEW JERSEY

BERRY BEST FARM, INC.
Goat Hill Rd.
Lambertville, NJ 08530
609-397-0748
Fresh raspberries, strawberries, and blackberries supplied to New York, New Jersey, and Pennsylvania. Also producers of a line of fine jams under the Coryell's Crossing label.

CHEESE JUNCTION
1 West Ridgewood Ave.
Ridgewood, NJ 07450
201-445-9211
Freshly cut gourmet cheeses and coffees. Catalog is $1, credited to first order.

THE CHINESE KITCHEN
P.O. Box 218, Dept. OC
Stirling, NJ 07980
201-665-2234
Mail-order source for Asian cooking supplies, cookbooks, utensils, spices, condiments, and gift items. Catalog subscription plus three recipes and a money-back coupon, $2.

D'ARTAGNAN, INC.
399 St. Paul Ave.
Jersey City, NJ 07306
201-792-0748
Domestic duck foie gras, raw and prepared fatted ducks, game birds, game, fresh galantines of foie gras, confit, smoked duck breast, smoked chicken, and other prepared items made from game and game birds.

JUGTOWN MOUNTAIN SMOKEHOUSE
P.O. Box 366
Flemington, NJ 08822
201-782-2421
*Smoked ham, turkey, pheasant, duck,
and goose, nitrite-free bacon, and
smoked cheeses and sausages.*

M & S GOURMET SPECIALTY FOODS
P.O. Box 3397
Teaneck, NJ 07666
201-833-9490
*Poultry smoked specifically for each
order (chicken, quail, pheasant, etc.),
smoked meats and fish, pâté, truffles, foie
gras, and cèpes.*

NEW YORK

BALDUCCI'S
424 Avenue of the Americas
New York, NY 10011
212-673-2600
*Prime meats, caviar, smoked salmon,
pâtés, charcuterie, international cheeses,
imported chocolates, aged vinegars, extra
virgin olive oils, confections, prepared
foods, and spices.*

THE BIRKETT MILLS
263 Main St.
Penn Yan, NY 14527
315-536-3311
*Fancy quality
buckwheat and
wheat products,
including flours,
grains, and
pancake mixes.*

BREMEN HOUSE, INC.
220 East 86th St.
New York, NY 10028
212-288-5500
*Fine European chocolates, candies,
cakes, smoked meats, truffles, coffees,
health supplements, and beauty aids.*

CAVIARTERIA
29 East 60th St.
New York, NY 10022
212-759-7410; outside New York
City 800-221-1020
*Direct importers of Caspian caviar,
including the famed "Imperial." Also,
Scotch and Swedish salmon, foie gras,
American sturgeon caviar, salmon
caviar, and whitefish golden caviar.*

CHEESES OF ALL NATIONS
153 Chambers St.
New York, NY 10007
212-732-0752; 212-964-0024
*Hundreds of domestic and imported
cheeses expertly cut just before shipping.
Catalog is $1.*

COMMONWEALTH ENTERPRISES LTD.
P.O. Box 49
Mongaup Valley, NY 12762
914-583-6630
Fresh Moulard foie gras.

DEAN & DELUCA
110 Greene St.
New York, NY 10012
212-431-1691; outside New York
City 800-221-7714
*Cheeses, smoked meats and fish, caviar,
oils, vinegars, dried mushrooms, sauces,
mustards, pastas, grains, rices, beans,
herbs and spices, coffees and teas,
preserves, honeys, confections, baked
goods, and gift baskets. Also
kitchenware, dinnerware, flatware, and
books. Catalog available.*

DiCAMILLO BAKING COMPANY, INC.
811 Linwood Ave.
Niagara Falls, NY 14305
716-282-2341
*Double-baked biscuits, biscotti di vino
(wine biscuits), biscotti, angelica (Italian
crisp breads), biscotti formaggio,
focaccia, tortas, and many other Italian
baked specialties.*

FLYING FOODS INTERNATIONAL
43–43 Ninth St.
Long Island City, NY 11101
718-706-0820
*Specialists in quality foods, gourmet
delicacies, fresh fish and vegetables from
all over the world. Fresh game meats,
fruits, and fruit purées are also available.*

THE FORST'S
CPO Box 1000P
Kingston, NY 12401
914-331-3500
*Fresh frozen game birds, steaks, and a
complete stock of smoked hams and
turkeys.*

FRASER-MORRIS FINE FOODS
931 Madison Ave.
New York, NY 10021
212-988-6700
*Fine gourmet foods, spices, and other
delicacies.*

HOUSE OF SPICES
76–17 Broadway
Jackson Heights, NY 11373
718-476-1577
*Specializing in Indo-Pak groceries and
spices. A major item is Basmati rice.*

IDEAL CHEESE SHOP LTD.
1205 Second Ave.
New York, NY 10021
212-688-7579
*A fine selection of cheeses. Free catalog
available.*

INDIANA MARKET & CATERING
80 Second Ave.
New York, NY 10003
212-505-7290
*Country-style prepared foods, farm
produce, regional packaged products,
domestic cheeses, home-baked desserts,
and other specialty items.*

KATHLEEN'S COOKIES
43 North Sea Rd.
Southampton, NY 11968
516-283-7153
and
KATHLEEN'S BAKE SHOP
155 East 84th St.
New York, NY 10028
212-570-1515
*Fine selection of farm-style sweets,
including fresh-baked cookies, pies, and
crutchley cruller hearts.*

PAMELA KRAUSMANN'S NOTEBOOKS
Dept. 183
496 LaGuardia Pl.
New York, NY 10012
212-473-8002
*A collection of mail-order catalogs
featuring quality foods and stories about
the people who produce them. Catalogs,
$3.*

LE GOURMAND
Box 433, Rt. 22
Peru, NY 12972
518-643-2499
*Oil, vinegar, condiments, cane sugar,
and miscellaneous imported fancy foods,
including a full line of products for the
amateur pastry chef, all available at
discount prices.*

LILAC CHOCOLATES, INC.
120 Christopher St.
New York, NY 10014
212-242-7374
*Semisweet, bitter, milk, and white
chocolate for eating, cooking, and
baking.*

LITTLE RAINBOW CHÈVRE
Box 379
Rodman Rd.
Hillsdale, NY 12529
518-325-3351
*Producers of the finest of goat cheeses in
many varieties, fresh, aged, and blue.*

McARTHUR'S SMOKEHOUSE, INC.
Main St.
Millerton, NY 12546
518-789-4425
*Finest-quality hickory-smoked meats,
fowl, and fish items, as well as a line of
specialty condiments.*

MAISON E. H. GLASS, INC.
52 East 58th St.
New York, NY 10022
212-755-3316
*Caviar, foie gras, truffles, Smithfield
hams, smoked salmon, imported cheeses,
deluxe chocolates, freshly roasted nuts,
gift baskets, and the world's largest
selection of epicurean specialties. Send
$5 to Dept. ACC for illustrated catalog.*

MANGANARO FOODS, INC.
488 Ninth Ave.
New York, NY 10018
212-563-5331; 212-563-5332
*A complete line of imported Italian
delicacies. Free catalog available.*

MONEO & SONS, INC.
CASA MONEO
210 West 14th St.
New York, NY 10011
212-929-1644
*Spanish, Mexican,
and Latin American
foods, condiments,
and spices.*

MR. SPICEMAN
615 Palmer Rd.
Yonkers, NY 10701
914-961-7776
*A full selection of both rare and common
spices, herbs, and flavorings. Large
savings on 1-pound sizes. Catalog is $1,
which is deductible from the first order.*

PAPRIKAS WEISS IMPORTER
1546 Second Ave.
New York, NY 10028
212-288-6117
Hungarian sweet paprika, spices, strudel dough, coffees, teas, baking ingredients, freshly ground nuts, pâtés, foie gras, salamis, sausages, cheeses, and cookware.

ROSSEYA GARDENS
853 North Main St.
Spring Valley, NY 10977
914-354-2440
Growers and shippers of elephant garlic.

SAMAKI, INC.
P.O. Box 4009
West Brookville, NY 12785
914-754-8340
A large variety of smoked products, including salmon, trout, sturgeon, Pacific tunny (tuny), mackerel, and Norwegian salmon.

SCHAPIRA COFFEE COMPANY
117 West 10th St.
New York, NY 10011
212-675-3733
Fresh coffees roasted daily.

SELECT ORIGINS, INC.
Box N
Southampton, NY 11968
516-288-1382
Fine-quality cooking ingredients from wild mushrooms to European chocolate in addition to a line of premium herbs and spices. A cooking newsletter and a supplement of seasonal offerings are included with the catalog.

THE SILVER PALATE
274 Columbus Ave.
New York, NY 10023
212-799-6340
Over 110 products using the Silver Palate's own recipes to create honest Country food with just a bit of city style.

SIMPSON & VAIL, INC.
P.O. Box 309
38 Clinton St.
Pleasantville, NY 10570
914-747-1336
Thirty-four black, Oolong, and green teas, plus 21 flavored teas. Coffees include a fancy Vienna roast, a decaffeinated Colombian coffee, and a decaffeinated espresso. Also available are specialty food items, such as peppercorns, bouquet garni, marmalade, mustards, and chocolates.

THOUSAND ISLANDS APIARIES
R.D. 2, Box 212
Clayton, NY 13624
315-654-2741
The finest flavored clover honey available in liquid form, as well as honey creams, both plain or flavored with maple sugar or cinnamon. Also comb honey, honey pots, candles, and gift samplers.

NORTH CAROLINA

MARIA'S
111 Stratford Rd.
Winston-Salem, NC 27104
919-722-7271
Fresh coffees roasted daily. Also a complete line of bulk spices and herbs, teas, fruits, nuts, cheeses, specialty foods, and gift baskets. Free catalog.

MORAVIAN SUGAR CRISP COMPANY, INC.
Rt. 2
Clemmons, NC 27012
919-764-1402
Hand-rolled and hand-cut Moravian cookies in five flavors, including lemon, ginger, and chocolate.

NUTS D'VINE
P.O. Box 589
Edenton, NC 27932
919-482-2222; out of state
800-334-0492
Gourmet peanuts in the shell, shelled, and water blanched. True cold-pressed virgin peanut oil is also available.

OHIO

BICKFORD FLAVORS
282 South Main St.
Akron, OH 44308
216-762-4666
All-natural, nonalcoholic flavors for cooking and baking, such as vanilla, maple, nutmeg, coconut, clove, peach, raspberry, and root beer. Sixty flavors to choose from.

CLIFTON MILL
75 Water St.
Clifton, OH 45316
513-767-5501
Whole and stone-ground grains, yellow cornmeal.

LAVIN'S MEATS
6428 Union Ave.
Alliance, OH 44601
216-871-4136
Gourmet hams and steaks cured and aged according to traditional Amish recipes.

SUGARDALE FOODS, INC.
Special Markets Division
1600 Harmont Ave. N.E.
P.O. Box 8440
Canton, OH 44711
216-455-5253
Gift food packages, such as hams, steaks, candy, honey, preserves, cookies, and nuts.

OREGON

CASCADE CONSERVES
P.O. Box 8306
Portland, OR 92707
503-224-6366; 503-224-8370
Conserves, low in sugar, made from premium-quality Oregon-Washington berries. Cooked in small quantities in copper kettles. Rare varieties such as huckleberry, black currant, nectarberry, wild mountain blackberry, and kumquat marmalade are available.

THE COFFEE, TEA & SPICE COMPANY
318 S.E. Baseline
Hillsboro, OR 97123
503-640-6522
Free catalog featuring specialty foods from the Pacific Northwest as well as culinary herbs and spices and gourmet coffees and teas.

FILBERTREATS
356 N.W. First Ave.
Canby, OR 97013
503-266-8172
Dipped filberts and fine filbert candies, including chocolate buttercreams, mints, and barks.

GRANDMA MORGAN'S
P.O. Box 972
Lake Oswego, OR 97034
503-293-3383
Items unique to the Pacific Northwest prepared by a small cottage industry.

JAKE'S FAMOUS PRODUCTS, INC.
4910 N. Basin
Portland, OR 97217
503-226-1420
Offering the same quality foods as served in Jake's restaurants in the Pacific Northwest. Some items available are smoked salmon, kippered salmon, salmon pâté, trout pâté, smoked white sturgeon, Alaska shrimp, cocktail and tartar sauces, and chocolate truffle cakes.

PINNACLE ORCHARDS
441 South Fir St.
Medford, OR 97501
503-772-6271
Juicy pears and apples grown in the famous Rogue River valley. Free catalog upon request.

S & H ORGANIC ACRES
P.O. Box 757
Red Hills Rd.
Newberg, OR 97132
503-538-6530
Elephant garlic and four other varieties of garlic, shallots, and onions. Write for free catalog.

THE STASH TEA COMPANY
P.O. Box 610AC
Portland, OR 97207
503-227-5077
All-natural herbal, caffeine-free, traditional, and black teas blended in Oregon. Also natural jams, preserves, and honeys.

WESTNUT
P.O. Box 125
Dundee, OR 97115
503-538-2161
Raw whole hazelnuts, as well as sliced, diced, and roasted hazelnuts for mail order.

PENNSYLVANIA

MRS. DE WILDT
R.D. 3
Bangor, PA 18013
215-588-1042
Distributors of rare spices and herbs. Specializing in Indonesian and other Asian foods, as well as Holland cheeses, bakery goods, and other gourmet specialties. Free catalog upon request.

THE DILWORTHTOWN COUNTRY STORE
275 Brintons Bridge Rd.
West Chester, PA 19382
215-399-0560
A line of specialty foods, including homemade preserves, jams, imported English condiments, and locally made foodstuffs. Some kitchenware is also available, such as custom-made cookie cutters in primitive designs, log cabin molds, and heart-shaped muffin pans.

GOURMAIL, INC.
Box 516
Berwyn, PA 19312
215-296-4620
Manufacturer and mail-order supplier of fancy foods and ingredients of India. Spices, sauces, specialty teas for Indian cooking.

THE GREAT VALLEY MILLS
687 Mill Rd.
Telford, PA 18969
215-256-6648
Specializing in stone-ground flours and grains and pancake and muffin mixes. Smoked meats and other Pennsylvania Dutch gourmet foods are also available.

JAMISON FARM
R.D. 2, Box 402
Latrobe, PA 15650
412-834-7424
Quality lamb naturally raised and grain-finished. All meat is cut to order, frozen, and shipped via UPS.

WALNUT ACRES, INC.
Penns Creek, PA 17862
717-837-0601
Organic foods.

WILBUR CHOCOLATES
Candy Americana Museum & Candy Outlet
48 North Broad St.
Lititz, PA 17543
717-626-1131
Quality chocolate, milk and dark coatings, pastel and white confectioners' coatings, and cookie chocolate drops. Send self-addressed, stamped envelope for price list.

YOUNDT'S COUNTRY SMOKEHOUSE
R.D. #1
Ephrata, PA 17522
717-738-2551
Pennsylvania Dutch foods by mail, including hams, bacon, scrapple, dried beef, jams and jellies, chow chow, cheeses, pretzels, apple butter, and apple schnitz.

SOUTH CAROLINA

EUGENE PLATT'S FISH COMPANY
Atlantis Sturgeon Caviar Dept.
714 Sea Mountain Highway
North Myrtle Beach, SC 29582
803-249-3711; 803-249-2008
Fresh Atlantic sturgeon caviar.

TENNESSEE

EARLY'S HONEY STAND
P.O. Drawer K
Springhill, TN 37174
615-486-2230
Regional smoked meats, including smoked turkey, smoked turkey breast, country ham, smoked ham, smoked bacon, and sausage. Mail-order service available through catalog.

TEXAS

CAP RANCH MEAT MARKET SMOKEHOUSE
Rt. 2, Box 269
Mineola, TX 75773
214-569-2822
Smoked turkey, ham, bacon, chicken, and German sausages.

CAVIAR EXPRESS
6519 Wrenwood Dr.
Dallas, TX 75252
214-985-7599
Fine imported and domestic caviars, smoked fish, foie gras, and other gourmet food specialties.

COLLIN STREET BAKERY
Box 79
Corsicana, TX 75110
214-872-3951
Freshly baked, hand-decorated deluxe fruitcake.

EILENBERGER'S BAKERY
512 North John St.
P.O. Box 710
Palestine, TX 75801
214-SAY-CAKE (729-2253)
Old-fashioned pecan cakes, fruitcakes, and Australian apricot cakes.

SAN FELIPE MESQUITE CHARCOAL COMPANY, INC.
1100 Montana Ave., Suite 203
El Paso, TX 79902
915-542-3875
Specializing in gourmet mesquite charcoal for home or restaurant use.

THE ZEYS OF TEXAS
P.O. Box 1048
Mission, TX 78572
512-585-8383
Mail-order Texas tree-ripened ruby red grapefruit and oranges, Texas pecans, and smoked meat products.

VERMONT

BROWN & JENKINS TRADING COMPANY
431-9 Pine St.
P.O. Box 1570
Burlington, VT 05402
802-862-2395
Fine gourmet coffees both whole bean and ground, as well as coffee-making accessories.

CAMPBELL FARMS
P.O. Box 74
Post Mills, VT 05058
802-333-4072
Suckling pig, either fresh or smoked. Also gourmet jams and jellies.

CHAMPLAIN CHOCOLATE COMPANY
431 Pine St.
Burlington, VT 05401
802-864-1807
All-handmade chocolates including American chocolate truffle, evergreen mint, honey caramel, maple crunch, and the Green Mountain.

CROWLEY CHEESE, INC.
Healdville, VT 05758
802-259-2340
Handmade cheese with no additives or preservatives.

THE DAKIN FARM
Rt. 7
Ferrisburg, VT 05456
802-425-3971
Pure Vermont maple syrup, smoked meats, aged Cheddar cheese.

GREEN MOUNTAIN SUGAR HOUSE
R.F.D. #1
Ludlow, VT 05149
802-228-7151
Maple syrup, maple candy, and maple cream as well as other Vermont products, such as cheeses, jams, and jellies.

LAWRENCE'S SMOKE HOUSE
Route 30, R.R. 1, Box 28
Newfane, VT 05345
802-365-7751
Corncob-smoked hams, bacon, poultry, fish, specialty meats, and cheeses. Write for brochure.

MAPLE GROVE FARMS OF VERMONT
167 Portland St.
Saint Johnsbury, VT 05819
802-748-5141
Pure maple syrup, pure granulated maple sugar, pure maple cream, Vermont salad dressings and barbecue sauce, and handmade confections. Free color catalog available.

PLYMOUTH CHEESE CORP.
Box 1
Plymouth, VT 05056
802-672-3650
Vermont cheeses, relishes, pickles, maple syrup, baked beans, brown bread, Indian pudding, and other gourmet specialties.

SHELBURNE FARMS
Shelburne, VT 05482
802-985-8686
Shelburne Farms Farmhouse Cheddar cheese.

THE STORE
Box 118, Rt. 100
Waitsfield, VT 05673
802-496-4465
Vermont preserves, foods, and antiques.

SUGARBUSH FARM CHEESE
R.F.D. 1, Box 568
High Pastures Rd.
Woodstock, VT 05091
802-457-1757
Extra-sharp natural Cheddar cheese, hickory- and maple-smoked cheese, sage cheese, Jack cheese, mellow Vermont Cheddar cheese, and blue cheese. Also pure Vermont maple syrup. Free catalog available.

HENRY & CORNELIA SWAYZE
Brookside Farm
Tunbridge, VT 05077
802-889-3738
Varieties of Vermont maple syrup.

WOOD'S CIDER MILL
R.F.D. #2, Box 266
Springfield, VT 05156
802-263-5547
Cider jelly, boiled cider, and maple syrup.

VIRGINIA

S. WALLACE EDWARDS & SONS, INC.
P.O. Box 25
Surry, VA 23883
804-294-3121; outside Virginia
800-222-4267
Genuine cured Virginia hams, bacon, and sausages. Write or call for free brochure.

FABULOUS FOODSTUFFS
1234 First St.
Dept. BK
Alexandria, VA 22314
703-836-5005
French butter, Parmesan, Cheddar, and other natural cheeses.

GWALTNEY OF SMITHFIELD LTD.
P.O. Box 489
Smithfield, VA 23430
804-357-3131
Cured and smoked Smithfield and Williamsburg brand hams, bacon, sausages, luncheon meats, franks, and fresh pork.

R & R LIMITED OF SMITHFIELD
P.O. Box 837
124 Main St.
Smithfield, VA 23430
804-357-5730
Smithfield hams and bacon, Virginia peanuts and preserves, and selected gift items.

SMITHFIELD PACKING CO.
P.O. Box 447
Smithfield, VA 23430
804-357-4321
Genuine Smithfield hams and country cured hams and bacon. Hams are sold either cooked or uncooked.

SUMMERFIELD FARM PRODUCTS LTD.
Rt. 1, Box 43
Boyce, VA 22620
703-837-1718
Producers of true milk-fed veal. Baby spring lambs and free-range chickens are also available.

TEEL MOUNTAIN FARM
Rt. 1, Box 411
Stanardsville, VA 22973
804-985-7608
Natural organic whole chickens and chicken parts.

WASHINGTON

DELAURENTI ITALIAN & INTERNATIONAL FOOD MARKETS
1435 First Ave.
Seattle, WA 98101
206-622-0141
Specialty foods and wines from around the world.

HEGG & HEGG SMOKED SALMON, INC.
801 Marine Dr.
Port Angeles, WA 98362
800-435-3474
Smoked salmon and seafood gift boxes and baskets.

MOTHER SPERRY'S PLUM PUDDING
1416 East Aloha St.
Seattle, WA 98112
206-329-8631
An old-fashioned, handmade dessert with no preservatives but plenty of dried fruit and good brandy. Available in three sizes.

PIKE PLACE MARKET
Seattle, WA 98101
Oldest operating farmers' market in the United States, includes four fish markets, a variety of specialty food stores, and thirty-five restaurants. Produce from all over the world sold year-round. Summer hours: Monday to Saturday, 9:00 A.M. to 6:00 P.M., Sunday, 11:00 A.M. to 5:00 P.M. Winter hours: Monday to Saturday, 9:00 A.M. to 6:00 P.M.

WAX ORCHARDS
Rt. 4, Box 320
Vashon, WA 98070
206-463-9735; 206-682-8251
Gourmet fruit juices, preserves, conserves, toppings, fruit butters, chutneys, and sauces.

WASHINGTON, D.C.

WICKENS AND HICKS AMERICAN STORE
1455 Pennsylvania Ave.
Washington, D.C. 20004
202-347-8880
A variety of herb plants and topiaries, as well as new and antique linens. Hand-painted dinnerware also available.

WISCONSIN

CHEESE 'N' MORE, INC.
8100 Highway K South
Merrill, WI 54452
715-675-6145
Featuring over 100 varieties of cheese.

FERRIS FINE FOODS, LTD.
P.O. Box 5412
Madison, WI 53705
608-233-2238
Top-quality Wisconsin cheeses, as well as a line of three sausages.

MODERN PRODUCTS, INC.
P.O. Box 09398
Milwaukee, WI 53209
414-352-3333
All-natural blended seasonings including vegit, onion magic, herbal bouquet, spike, lemon pepper, and Indo meat tenderizer.

NORTHWESTERN COFFEE MILLS
217 North Broadway
Milwaukee, WI 53202
414-276-1031
Imported coffees, teas, and spices.

NUESKE HILLCREST FARM MEATS
R.R. 2
Wittenberg, WI 54499
715-253-2226; outside Wisconsin
800-38-BACON; in Wisconsin
800-37-BACON
Finest-quality ham, bacon, and sausages, smoked naturally over an open applewood fire.

SMITH BROTHERS
100 North Franklin St.
Port Washington, WI 53074
414-284-5592
American caviar, black, red, and golden whitefish caviar, smoked fish, such as chub, salmon, and trout.

THE SWISS CHEESE SHOP
Highway 69 North
P.O. Box 429
Monroe, WI 53566
608-325-3493
Aged Wisconsin cheese. Available by mail only.

USINGER'S FAMOUS SAUSAGE
1030 North Third St.
Milwaukee, WI 53203
414-276-9100
Makers of over seventy-five varieties of Old World sausages. A selection of gift boxes is also available. Write or call for free brochure.

VILLAGE CHEESE
507 East Silver Spring
Milwaukee, WI 53217
414-962-3110
Wisconsin cheeses, gourmet coffees, Clearbrook Farms preserves, and Judy and Toby's sugar-free preserves. Gift packages are available.

WISCONSIN FISHING COMPANY/ FISHER BROTHERS FISHERIES, INC.
P.O. Box 965
Green Bay, WI 54305
414-437-3582
Quality seafood, including shrimp, lobster, crab, oysters, scallops, fish steaks, herring, smoked fish, breaded and battered fish and seafood, and seafood sauce mixes.

MENU

Holiday Punch

*Crudités and
Parsley-Chive Dip*
page 47

*Salmon in
Champagne Sauce*

Green Beans with Cashews

*Wild Rice and Brown Rice
with Mushrooms*

*Crunchy Oat and
Cranberry Muffins*

*Washington State
Apple Cake*

*The buffet dinner is highlighted
by king salmon served whole in
an old dough bowl lined with
parsley, sage, rosemary, and
thyme (above). A bird's nest
manger stands amid antique
pewter on the mantel. The
welcoming wreath (left) on
the front door was assembled
from grapevines, dried herbs,
and fresh holly.*

HOLIDAY PUNCH

Gaye likes to freeze this punch until it's slushy, though it's just as good served very cold.

1 cup sugar
1 46-ounce can unsweetened pineapple juice
1 12-ounce can frozen orange juice concentrate, thawed
1 tablespoon fresh lemon juice
1 1.5-liter bottle Soave or other dry white wine
4 cups ice water
3 ripe bananas

In a very large bowl, combine all of the ingredients, except the bananas. Stir very well until the sugar has dissolved. Pour the mixture into a large container and freeze until icy and thick.

Serve from a punch bowl, with thinly sliced bananas on top.

Makes about 2 dozen 6-ounce servings

SALMON IN CHAMPAGNE SAUCE

The king salmon Gaye purchased at the Pike Place Market was 30 inches long. The recipe has been adjusted for the salmon you and I might find in our markets.

Laid out in a mosaic of colors on a wood tray, the crudités match the eye appeal of the blue-and-white Canton punch service, a popular collectible in English households of the 19th century.

1 whole 6- to 8-pound salmon, dressed
6 shallots, minced
1 pound fresh mushrooms, chopped, with 10 mushroom caps reserved
1 25.4-ounce bottle nonvintage Champagne or sparkling wine
1 teaspoon fresh lemon juice
1¾ cups crème fraîche or heavy cream
4 tablespoons (½ stick) unsalted butter
Salt and freshly ground black pepper
Bunches of fresh herbs, for garnish

Preheat the oven to 450°F. Generously butter a large baking dish or fish poacher and place the salmon in it. Add the shallots and mushrooms and pour the Champagne over all.

Bake the salmon, uncovered, basting from time to time, for about 45 minutes, or until just cooked through.

Meanwhile, poach the reserved mushroom caps in about 1 cup of water and the lemon juice. Remove and set aside to drain.

When it is cooked, remove the salmon from the pan and set it aside. Strain the cooking liquid into a heavy saucepan, reserving the shallots and mushrooms. Boil the liquid over high heat until it is reduced to about ½ cup. Add the crème fraîche and boil until the sauce is reduced and thickened.

Cut the butter into bits and whisk it into the sauce, one piece at a time, until emulsified. Season with salt and pepper to taste. Skin the salmon and place it on a platter. Pour the sauce over and garnish with bunches of fresh herbs and the poached mushroom caps.

Serves 8